G000272706

THE CRAFT OF ENAMELLING

THE BOOK

This book offers a series of projects which encourage the learner by giving him 'something to show' for his efforts right from the start. New techniques (some of them developed by the author to an unusual extent) are gradually introduced in a logical sequence, and the more advanced or gifted pupil is given plenty of opportunity to develop his abilities. (Details of objects to be made and processes involved can be seen in the List of Contents.) Verbal instructions are amply supplemented by clear, well-planned diagrams, and the standard of design is high. The lively and accomplished work in the photographs all done by secondary schoolboys, speaks for itself.

It is assumed that the student will already know the basic processes of metalwork including the names and functions of the most commonly used tools. Given this basis of knowledge, the book is suitable for school classes or for the older beginner who finds in craft enamelling a satisfying hobby.

THE AUTHOR

Kenneth Neville entered the teaching profession in 1957 after fifteen years in industry.

On obtaining his Full Technological Certificate he continued with his studies as a part-time student at Burnley School of Art, where he took a general art course including pottery. Using his knowledge of ceramics and metalwork he combined the two in the form of enamelling of metal to bring a more creative approach to the teaching of metalwork.

He has held teacher courses on enamelling for several Education Authorities and Youth Organizations and in other types of further education.

He is a craft member of the Bluecoat Display Centre and his work in the field of wood sculpture has been exhibited at several exhibitions including those of the Red Rose Guild of Craftsmen.

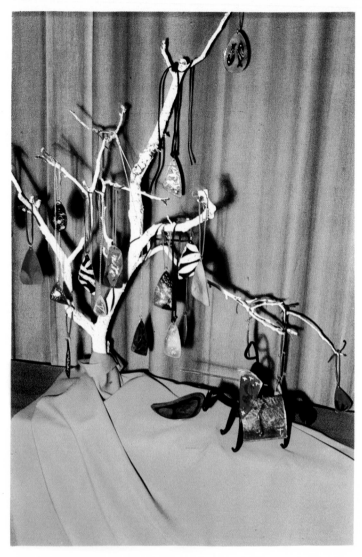

The knight (mild steel with enamel) rides towards a tree hung with pendants of various types

THE CRAFT OF
ENAMELLING

Kenneth Neville

Head of Handicraft Dept, Padiham County Secondary School
Craft Lecturer, Lancashire Education Authority

with illustrations by the author

 MILLS & BOON, LONDON

First published 1966 by Mills & Boon Limited, 50 Grafton Way,
Fitzroy Square, London W.1

© *Kenneth Neville 1966*

Reprinted 1968
Reprinted (with revisions) 1970

ISBN 0 263 51654 7

Printed in Great Britain
by Jarrold & Sons Ltd, Norwich

Contents

CONTENTS

List of Plates

9

Acknowledgments

All the work photographed in this book was done by boys at
Padiham County Secondary School, and my thanks are due to my
Headmaster, Mr D. Senogles, B.SC., and the Governors of the
School for permission to include them in my book.

My thanks also to Mr F. Wood, Works Manager, and Mr F.
Gibson, Works Supervisor of Blake Vitreous Enamellers; Mr. W.
G. Ball and Mr R. Ball of W. G. Ball Ltd, Enamel Manufacturers;
Mr K. Phipps, Technical Manager of Metal Porcelains Ltd;
Mr D. Davidson of Ferro Enamels; Mr A. Wilkinson, Handicraft
Organizer for Lancashire; Mr Thornton, A.R.C.A., F.R.S.A., and the
staff of Burnley School of Art whose tuition and encouragement
made the writing of this book possible.

To my many friends and colleagues for their constructive
criticism of my work.

K.N.

Introduction

ENAMELLING is not a new craft. Evidence of its use dates back to 1500 B.C. The early Egyptians used enamel as a glaze for bricks and pottery. Nearer to home the Celts were pouring enamel into bronze shapes. The earliest British enamels belong to the sixth to ninth century B.C.

The craft of enamelling began to decline at the turn of the century with the introduction of mass-produced enamelled domestic appliances. In the early thirties the Americans began to revive it as a craft, and today it has a wide following of craftsmen turning out individual pieces for collectors and architectural purposes.

Enamelling is a fascinating craft covering a variety of techniques and skills, ranging from simple copper jewellery to larger types of enamel-work such as coffee-table-tops and murals.

Very little work has been done in the use of enamel as a medium for the school craft-rooms and Art departments. With the introduction of enamelling into Handicraft-rooms you have available the three basic fundamentals of design: line, form, and colour. Line and form have always been available in the use of rod, bar, sheet, and timber. Colour has only been available with the use of synthetic paint or the forming of oxides on the surface of the metal. By using enamel you have a permanent coloured surface that will withstand the elements if necessary.

As a medium for the Art department, enamel has a brilliance and depth of colour that is unsurpassed by any other medium. It offers limitless possibilities as a means of creating textures and patterns of colour.

This book has been written with the intention of introducing a creative approach to the teaching of metalwork, and for the craft enthusiast who works at home with limited equipment.

The cost of craft enamelling is not high. Small kilns are available at reasonable prices, and propane and butane gas cylinders and torches are readily available for those who have no brazing equipment and wish to fire enamel.

The skills required for enamelling cover the whole educational field. For the slower type of child it offers the opportunity of being able to say 'I too will something make, and joy in the making', while it gives excellent scope to the more advanced type of pupil.

One of the advantages of enamelling with lower forms is that they can see the results of their labour very quickly; the time required for firing an enamel being only two or three minutes. The end result is acceptable by both the maker and his parents and is comparable to any article that can be purchased in the shops.

With this in mind I have compiled a series of projects in the form of a visual aid, and by working through these projects you are introduced to the various techniques and application of enamel that are available to you.

All the projects in this book have been made by my pupils in a secondary modern school situated in an industrial area of Lancashire. No doubt when you have acquired the techniques you will have your own interpretation of the use of enamel.

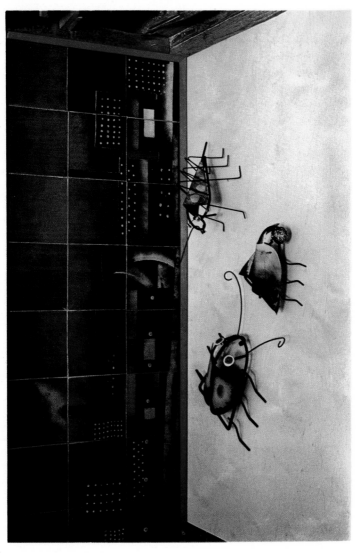

Science fiction take-over by giant insects? No—the 'window view' in the background is a mural, made of enamelled steel tiles and portraying a local industrial scene

1: *What is Enamel?*

OVER the last few years the term enamel has been generally associated with synthetic paint for household use. This should not be confused with vitreous enamel, which is the fusion of glass on to a metal background.

There are four types of jewellery enamel: opaque, transparent, opalescent, and translucent, and these are available from the manufacturers in cake form or already ground ready for use. This ground enamel is called frit and is purchased in different degrees of fineness.

The enamels have for their base a transparent, colourless glass called flux, which is composed of silica, red lead, and potash. This is made in different degrees of hardness depending on the composition; those containing more lead and potash are the softer and more brilliant.

Colours are obtained by the addition of metallic oxides to the flux. Opacity is obtained by the inclusion of oxides of lead and tin.

The constituents for the jewellery enamels are smelted in small quantities of 5 lb. to 7 lb. in special fireclay crucibles at 1150° C to 1250° C, and poured out on to metal slabs in cake form about ½ inch in thickness. They are then crushed and ground dry.

It will be seen by looking at the manufacturers' catalogues that by the skilful blending of these oxides with the flux, hundreds of colours are available for the enamellist.

Steel enamels are basically composed of borax, felspar, and quartz with antimony, titanium, or zirconium added for opacity.

The manufacture of steel enamels differs from the manufacture of jewellery enamels in respect of quantity. The constituents of enamel are melted in a furnace with a capacity of ½ ton or more. The molten enamel is then discharged from the furnace in a controlled stream into a tank of cold water, which immediately cools and shatters the enamel into small fragments.

The fragments of enamel or frit are then dried and cleaned and fed into hoppers to await distribution.

Enamels for aluminium are now available, but due to the low melting-point required there is only a limited range of colours.

Typical Jewellery Enamel Formula

Quartz	33
Red lead	33
Borax	9
Sodium carbonate	12
Calcium carbonate	3
Barium carbonate	3
Potassium nitrate	7
	100

Plus colouring oxides such as cobalt oxide for blue, copper oxide for turquoise, gold powder for ruby, etc.

Typical Steel Enamel Formula

SHEET IRON GROUND COATS

Borax	39 to 42%
Felspar	19 to 21%
Quartz	28 to 30%
Soda ash	7 to 9%
Sodium nitrate	3·4 to 3·8%
Fluorspar	3·4 to 4·3%
Cobalt oxide	0·2 to 0·4%
Nickel oxide	1·5 to 1·8%
Manganese oxide	0·3 to 0·8%

SHEET IRON COVER COATS

Borax	23 to 26%
Felspar	13 to 15%
Quartz	33 to 36%
Soda ash	9 to 13%
Sodium nitrate	7 to 9%
Titanium oxide	5 to 7%
Sodium antimonate	8 to 10%
Sodium silicofluoride	8 to 9%
Calcium phosphate	2 to 4%

3 *Pouring molten enamel on to a steel slab*

Types of metal suitable for enamelling

COPPER

Copper is the ideal metal for enamelling, especially for schools or for the beginner in the craft. It is available in sheet, bar, rod, tube, wire, and mesh. Being malleable and ductile, copper in sheet form can be cut very easily with hand-shears and beaten into shape with a mallet. In wire form it can be drawn through drawplates to various thicknesses and sections.

GILDING METAL

The enamelling of gilding metal can be successful, provided the metal is not subjected to more than two firings. Any prolonged heating causes the zinc in the metal to burn out, causing imperfections and discoloration in the enamel.

SILVER

For the successful enamelling of silver, fine silver or enamelling silver should be used. This has a melting-point of 960° C and can be purchased in similar forms as copper.

Sterling silver can be enamelled, but due to the silver being alloyed with copper the melting-point is lower, 875° C. As this is very near to the fusion-point of some enamels care must be taken on choice of enamels, otherwise the silver will collapse. There is also the problem of imperfections and pitting of the surface of the enamel if several firings are required.

GOLD

Many fine examples of enamelling on gold are to be found in churches and museums, giving evidence of the fine craftsmanship put into the art of enamelling in combination with gold. Due to the prohibitive price of gold today very little work is done in gold outside the jewellery trade.

STEEL

The enamelling of steel has progressed from the middle of the last century until today thousands of domestic appliances are manufactured with vitreous enamel surfaces. Mild steel sheet can be enamelled, but for the little extra cost it is preferable to use enamelling steel, as the enamelling of mild steel could lead to defects such as copperheading or blistering, due to the evolution of gases when the steel is heated.

ALUMINIUM

Today there are interesting developments in the field of vitreous enamelling aluminium. Enamelled aluminium has the advantage of being light in weight, resistant to corrosion, and flexible.

The aluminium suitable for enamelling is classified as N.S. 98, but due to the many snags that can arise it has its limitations in the craft field at the present time. No doubt in the very near future aluminium will take its place alongside other metals that have been enamelled, and it is in the architectural field that it will find a ready-made market.

Preparation of copper, gilding metal, silver for enamelling

The surface of the metal must be perfectly clean, and it requires the removal of grease and oxides to ensure adhesion of the enamel.

DEGREASING

The metal can be degreased by an abrasive, a detergent, or by grease burning.

ABRASIVES

The metal should be placed on a paper towel and scrubbed with pumice-powder, steel-wool, or 'Scotchbrite' abrasive-pad. I find the abrasive-pad to be most suitable for this method, because there is no danger of particles of steel-wool being fired into an enamel.

Rinse the metal under water; do not touch the surface with your fingers because the grease would transfer on to the metal and prevent the fusion of the enamel.

GREASE BURNING

The removal of grease by grease burning is the most efficient method for the craft-room.

Heat the metal in the kiln or by means of a torch until dull red. Remove the metal with brass tongs and quench in water, then, still holding the metal with the tongs, place in the pickle-bath.

REMOVAL OF OXIDES

The method used for removing oxides from the metal is the use of dilute acid. This operation is known as 'pickling'.

PICKLE-BATH

A pickle-bath comprises 10 parts water and 1 part sulphuric acid.

The container should be either glass, earthenware, or lead lined. For small jewellery-work a 'Pyrex' dish is ideal. In the school craft-room a container with a well-fitting lid is to be recommended, with 'Acid-Bath' clearly marked on the side.

Pour the water in the bath first and slowly add the acid to the water. It is quite safe adding acid to a bulk of water.

Do not add water to acid as this creates a violent reaction and could result in burning with spurting acid.

Use rubber gloves when pouring acid from the bottle into the dry glass measure and for pouring into the acid-bath.

Another safety measure is to fill the pickle-bath only half-way. This prevents the acid spilling over the sides when you place metal in the bath and remove it.

On removal from the pickle-bath, the copper should have a pink colour; this indicates complete removal of the oxides.

In schools this type of pickle-bath is a standard practice in the workshops for use by pupils, in preparing metal for beaten metalwork.

Should you find this pickle-bath undesirable you could make a bath for small work with vinegar and salt. Pour $\frac{1}{2}$ pint of vinegar into a container and add 1 dessertspoonful of table salt. The removal of oxides with this bath will take about 15 minutes.

RINSING

After the copper has been pickled it is necessary to remove the acid from the metal by rinsing in water. In schools the ideal position for the pickle-bath is under or near a sink. Should this not be possible, then you require a container of water to rinse the metal. Using tongs or tweezers, hold the metal vertical beneath the tap and allow water to run copiously on all sides.

In the event of any traces of oxides remaining on the copper, scrubbing with a brush and pumice-powder will generally remove them. Rinse again in water and dry on a paper towel.

Preparation of jewellery enamel

Enamel can be purchased from enamel suppliers either in cake form, crushed and washed, or ground ready for use. It is then known by the term 'frit'.

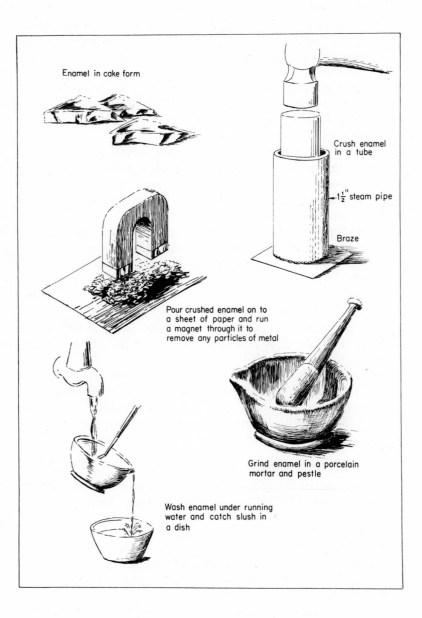

Enamel in cake form

Crush enamel in a tube

$1\frac{1}{2}''$ steam pipe

Braze

Pour crushed enamel on to a sheet of paper and run a magnet through it to remove any particles of metal

Grind enamel in a porcelain mortar and pestle

Wash enamel under running water and catch slush in a dish

CAKE FORM

The enamel in cake form is irregular in shape and approximately $\frac{1}{2}$ inch in thickness. To be suitable for use the enamel has to be crushed and then reduced to the consistency of table salt by means of a mortar and pestle.

The enamel can be crushed by wrapping in several layers of paper and striking with a hammer, or by placing one or two pieces in a tube and crushing with a round bar of hardened cast steel or case-hardened mild steel.

After crushing pour the enamel frit on to a clean paper and run a magnet through it to remove any particles of metal that may have contaminated the frit with crushing.

Place the crushed frit in a mortar and reduce further with a pestle until it will pass through a 60 mesh.

The frit should now be washed to remove any dust and dirt and to separate the finer particles of frit that tend to ball together.

Pour the frit into a dish and hold under a slow-running tap. Gently stir the frit with a spatula, causing the dirt to rise to the surface.

Allow this scum to overflow and be caught in a dish underneath.

Wash the frit until the water is no longer cloudy and place on a paper towel and allow to dry, on top of the kiln, or in a domestic cooker.

The finer particles of frit caught in your second dish should also be dried and kept in a separate container. This is known as slush enamel, and is suitable for use in counter-enamelling.

When the enamel is perfectly dry it should be stored in screw-top containers such as coffee-jars.

CRUSHED AND WASHED ENAMEL

Enamel can be purchased already crushed, and is suitable for decorative effects when fired on to enamelled surfaces and for the making of beads and eyes.

GROUND ENAMEL

Enamel frit can be purchased already ground ready for use at little extra cost. Opaque enamels are generally ground to pass 60 mesh and transparent enamels to pass 30 mesh.

The enamels are ground at the manufacturers' by means of a ball-mill which consists of a silica-lined cylinder that contains porcelain balls. Enamel is placed in the mill which slowly revolves the porcelain balls, grinding the enamel frit to the fineness required.

When your ground enamel arrives from the manufacturers it is necessary to wash your enamels prior to using to remove any dirt and dust through grinding.

It is important that the enamel frits are stored in screw-top containers and not left in the packets. This is necessary because the frits, especially the transparent frits, are liable to become cloudy and pitted when fired due to atmospheric contamination.

Preparation of gum

The gum that we use in school is pulverized gum tragacanth, which can be obtained from enamel suppliers, etching suppliers, or chemists.

To make the gum suitable for use, you require to take $\frac{1}{2}$ ounce of gum and mix to a creamy consistency with methylated spirits; add 1 quart of cold water; stir with a rod, and allow to stand overnight.

Another suitable adhesive, and one that is readily available, is 'Polycell' wallpaper adhesive. This only requires sprinkling in cold water and allowing to stand for 15 minutes. The gum should not be too thick, but about the consistency of stationery gum.

I have found that this is an ideal adhesive, as it burns away leaving no carbon deposit to contaminate the enamel.

Kilns and methods of firing enamel

FIRE ENAMELLING

Small copper brooches, pendants, and ashtrays about 5 inches in diameter can be successfully enamelled by means of a gas and air torch on the brazing hearth or by means of pressurized propane gas such as 'Calor' for those who have no brazing equipment.

You require a $\frac{1}{4}$-inch or $\frac{3}{8}$-inch wire mesh to support your copper shape, and this can be purchased under the name of 'Panning Metal' from enamel suppliers or it can be obtained from hardware-shops.

The size generally used is 1 foot square. It should be placed on a stand made from $\frac{1}{2}$-inch M.S. angle or supported on firebricks.

Fusion of the enamel is accomplished by directing the torch underneath the copper until the enamel becomes molten and perfectly smooth.

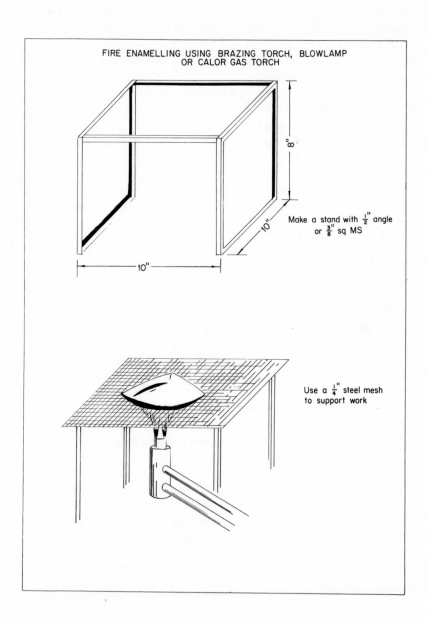

FIRE ENAMELLING USING BRAZING TORCH, BLOWLAMP
OR CALOR GAS TORCH

8"

10"

10"

Make a stand with $\frac{1}{2}$" angle
or $\frac{3}{8}$" sq MS

Use a $\frac{1}{4}$" steel mesh
to support work

Care must be taken that the flame is removed as soon as the enamel reaches this stage, otherwise you will experience a burning out of enamel round the edges, especially with flat shapes.

Burning out can be used to advantage with enamel-work, as I feel it does not detract from the charm of fire-enamelled work. Opaque reds tend to change to a dark brown, white will fire a beautiful green, and ivory will fire to an amber transparent. Transparent enamels such as blue will appear almost a pewter colour at the edges when over-fired.

One of the advantages with this simple and inexpensive method of firing enamel is that you can work the enamel in its molten stage and form decorative motifs by means of a wire.

KILNS

The kilns generally used today are electric because they have the advantage of heating quickly and have a good recovery of temperature after the kiln has been loaded. Temperature is controlled by means of a simmerstat switch.

The size of the kiln is another factor. Electric kilns are much smaller than the gas kilns and require no flue to disperse the fumes.

There are several kilns available, varying in size from $4 \times 4 \times 6$-inch muffle. Our largest kiln for craft-work has a $9 \times 9 \times 6$-inch muffle.

When purchasing a kiln for enamelling bear in mind the size of work you are likely to enamel. Make sure that the kiln has a safety-switch fitted to cut off the electricity supply when the kiln door is opened. Check that the time required to reach enamelling temperature, $800°$ C, is not too long. The kilns we use reach enamelling temperature in 1 hour 15 minutes.

PYROMETERS

Should you purchase a kiln for enamelling, then I recommend you buy a pyrometer to register temperature. This is essential if you fire several pieces of enamel such as tiles, because you must know the kiln temperature and fire for the same length of time, otherwise they will vary in colour.

ENAMELLING KITS

Available today are small electric enamelling kilns that consist of a flat element similar to the electric hot-plate on a cooker, plus enamels, gum, spatulas, copper shapes, etc. These kits are manufactured by Enamelaire (address on p. 151).

The enamels are fired by placing your copper shape in the centre of the hot-plate and covering with a 'Pyrex' dish.

These kilns are very simple and easy to use, but as they have a maximum temperature of 750°C, low-firing enamels have to be used. They are also restrictive in the size of metal that can be enamelled.

Methods of supporting enamel

At the present time of writing there are no kiln supports available for the enamellist. The ceramic stilts used by the potter are unsuitable for use in enamelling.

The supports that I use are very simple to make, and are made out of 'Nichrome' or stainless-steel sheet to withstand the temperature and prevent firescale forming.

The drawings on pages 27 and 28 are self-explanatory and the stilts should be made to suit the size and shape you intend to fire.

When firing articles that are enamelled on one side only, they can be placed on a stainless-steel mesh, which is placed in the kiln on triangular stainless-steel supports.

The mesh and large tiles are placed in the kiln by means of a fork 18 inches in length, made out of $\frac{3}{16}$-inch M.S. rod. Drill two $\frac{1}{8}$-inch holes in each prong and braze four $\frac{3}{4} \times \frac{1}{8}$-inch M.S. points into position.

A stand for firing steel tiles can be made by the welding of Perritt points on nickel-chrome bar. When making the stand allow for the prongs of the fork to enter the kiln.

Wire and small tubes can be easily supported by placing in holes drilled in refractory bricks. These bricks are easily cut with a hacksaw and should be drilled to suit your wire.

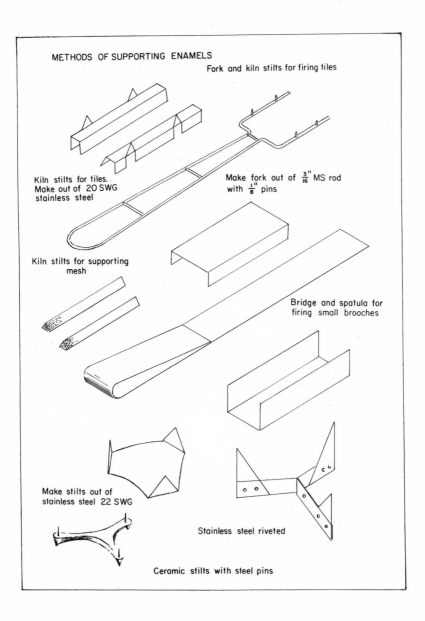

METHODS OF SUPPORTING ENAMELS

Fork and kiln stilts for firing tiles

Kiln stilts for tiles.
Make out of 20 SWG
stainless steel

Make fork out of $\frac{3}{16}''$ MS rod
with $\frac{1}{8}''$ pins

Kiln stilts for supporting
mesh

Bridge and spatula for
firing small brooches

Make stilts out of
stainless steel 22 SWG

Stainless steel riveted

Ceramic stilts with steel pins

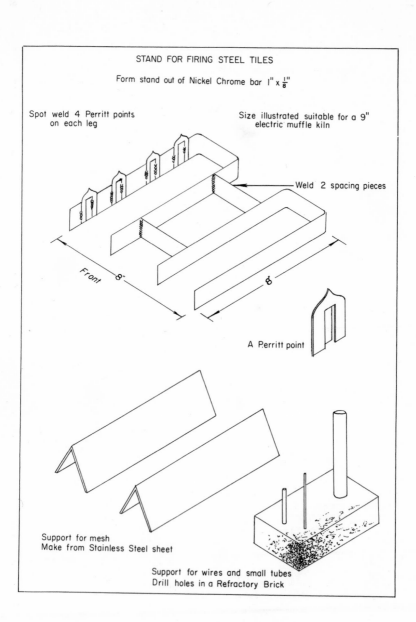

STAND FOR FIRING STEEL TILES

Form stand out of Nickel Chrome bar $1" \times \frac{1}{8}"$

Spot weld 4 Perritt points
on each leg

Size illustrated suitable for a 9"
electric muffle kiln

Weld 2 spacing pieces

Front   8"

9"

A Perritt point

Support for mesh
Make from Stainless Steel sheet

Support for wires and small tubes
Drill holes in a Refractory Brick

2: Enamelled Copper Brooch with Thread and Frit Decoration

THE making of a brooch with a simple decoration is a good starting-point for your enamelling.

The brooch described has for its decoration enamel threads and a small piece of frit. Alternative designs are at the rear of the book and the decoration can be one of several methods shown in further projects.

Draw your outline on a piece of copper $2 \times 1\frac{1}{4}$-inch $\times$ 20 SWG, and cut to shape, using hand-shears. If several brooches are to be made, by reversing the pattern on every other one the waste of copper would be negligible.

Place the copper in a vice and clean the edge with a file and emery-cloth. Protect the surface of the copper by using vice-grips.

If the brooch is slightly rounded it helps to give depth to the enamel, more than if it is just left as a flat surface.

By placing the copper on a slow curved stake and striking the edge with a planishing hammer, the copper will follow the contour of the stake.

The next stage is to degrease and deoxidize the copper ready for enamelling. (See Metal Preparation—also drawings on page 30.)

When the copper has been cleaned place on a clean sheet of paper and brush the surface with gum tragacanth.

Making shakers

These are made out of screw-top jars. Remove the cardboard packing from the screw top, and cut a hole in the centre of the top allowing a margin of $\frac{1}{4}$ inch round the edge. Cut a corresponding hole in the cardboard packing. The sieve is cut out of phosphor-bronze lawn. This can be purchased from suppliers of ceramic materials.

Lawns are manufactured in different sizes, the number of spaces to the linear inch being the size of mesh. The lawns generally used for dusting enamel are 60 and 100 mesh.

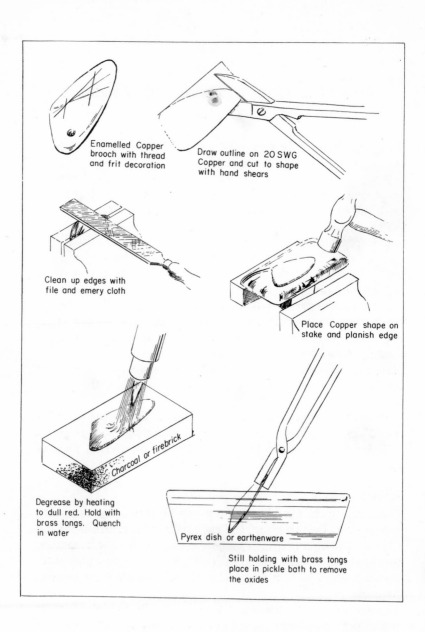

Enamelled Copper brooch with thread and frit decoration

Draw outline on 20 SWG Copper and cut to shape with hand shears

Clean up edges with file and emery cloth

Place Copper shape on stake and planish edge

Charcoal or firebrick

Degrease by heating to dull red. Hold with brass tongs. Quench in water

Pyrex dish or earthenware

Still holding with brass tongs place in pickle bath to remove the oxides

By using similar-type screw-top jars for storing ground enamel, it is only necessary to replace the top with one containing a mesh. This will cut down the risk of spilling and contaminating the enamel through transferring from one jar to another.

In the event of enamel becoming mixed with another type or colour, do not return it to its storage-jar: place the contaminated enamel in a separate jar. Enamel collected in this way can be used for counter-enamelling, which is discussed in Chapter 12. By dusting the multicoloured enamel on to brooches and small trays, unusual colour effects can be obtained.

Dusting the enamel

Dust the enamel on evenly, taking particular care the edges are covered and that there are no bare spots. Too thin a covering will result in the enamel burning out, and too thick a covering could result in the enamel cracking and flaking when cooling, due to the unequal expansion and contraction of enamel and metal. With practice you will soon acquire this technique of applying the right amount of enamel.

Now slide a spatula under the brooch and transfer it to a wire mesh or a trivet and place on top of your kiln and allow the gum to dry. If necessary you could increase the rate of drying by placing the brooch in the kiln for a few seconds and then withdrawing it.

Be sure that the gum has dried before firing or you will have a disappointing result due to moisture disturbing the enamel and causing pitting of the surface.

Firing

Jewellery enamels generally reach maturing-point around the 800° C mark. As there will be a drop in temperature of 50° C when the kiln is opened (this will vary with size and type of kiln) it is necessary to preheat the kiln to 850° C or bright red in appearance.

When the gum has dried hold a pair of tongs or firing fork in your right hand and grasp hold of the mesh. With your left hand open the door of the kiln and carefully place the mesh and brooch on the kiln supports. Remove the tongs and close the door. With a little practice this can be done in one flowing movement resulting in very little heat loss.

After a minute has passed check for the fusion of the enamel by means of the peephole in the kiln door.

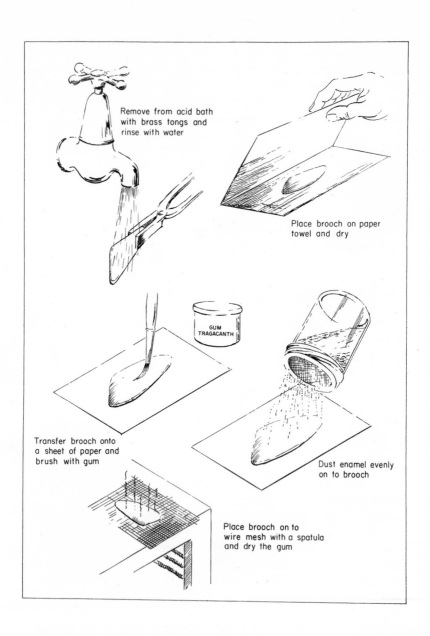

Remove from acid bath with brass tongs and rinse with water

Place brooch on paper towel and dry

GUM TRAGACANTH

Transfer brooch onto a sheet of paper and brush with gum

Dust enamel evenly on to brooch

Place brooch on to wire mesh with a spatula and dry the gum

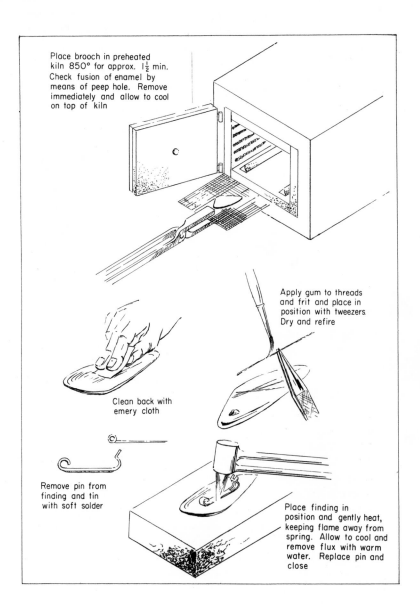

Place brooch in preheated kiln 850° for approx. 1½ min. Check fusion of enamel by means of peep hole. Remove immediately and allow to cool on top of kiln

Apply gum to threads and frit and place in position with tweezers. Dry and refire

Clean back with emery cloth

Remove pin from finding and tin with soft solder

Place finding in position and gently heat, keeping flame away from spring. Allow to cool and remove flux with warm water. Replace pin and close

33

The first stage of fusion is a darkening of the enamel; it then begins to become molten with an undulating surface and finally changes into a smooth reflecting surface.

Immediately the enamel has reached this maturing-point open the kiln door with your left hand, and, holding a pair of tongs with your right hand, remove the mesh and place on top of the kiln to cool.

Removing oxides

When the brooch has cooled the oxides should be removed from the back before further enamel is applied.

These can be removed by emery-cloth or by placing in the pickle-bath for a few minutes.

The decoration is in the form of enamel threads and a small piece of transparent frit. Paint the gum on the threads and frit and place in position with a pair of tweezers. Allow the gum to dry before firing. After the final firing the back must be cleaned once more to remove the oxides.

Soft soldering

Enamels that require pins, wire, clips, etc. soldered to their backs should not be subjected to the high temperatures necessary for hard soldering. Should you work in silver and require silver findings hard soldered to the back you should make a separate back and setting, and fit the enamel as a panel into the setting. (See Bezel Setting, page 81.)

They can, however, be soft soldered at 170°C with no harmful effect to the enamel.

Pins and findings suitable for soft soldering can be purchased at craft-shops and jewellers' merchants.

Remove the pin from the finding to prevent it from becoming annealed through heating. Coat the underneath surface with a flux such as 'Fluxite' or 'Baker's Soldering Fluid'. Hold the pin with pliers and heat with a small flame or soldering-iron and apply tinman's solder. Apply flux to the brooch and place the finding in position and gently heat, keeping the flame away from the spring. Immediately the solder flows, remove the torch and allow the brooch to cool. Remove any surplus flux from the back with warm water and replace the pin into the finding.

3: Trail Enamelling

THIS type of enamelling requires the decoration to be formed when the enamel is at the molten stage. Consequently it is only suitable for fire enamelling or with the use of the small hot-plate kiln where you can work on the enamelled surface.

By placing enamel threads and pieces of frit in various positions, and moving your wire through the molten enamel, numerous decorative motifs can be made.

Trail-enamelled brooch

To make a brooch in trail enamelling you require to cut your shape out of 20 SWG copper sheet with a pair of shears and tidy the edges with a file and emery-cloth.

The next stage is to degrease the copper by heating to a dull red with the torch, then quenching in water.

The oxides should then be removed by holding the copper with brass tongs and placing in the pickle-bath for a few minutes.

Remove from the pickle-bath and rinse under water, then dry with a paper towel. Do not touch the surface of the copper with your fingers.

Place the copper on a clean piece of paper, coat the surface with gum, and dust a transparent blue enamel evenly over the surface. Carefully place five or six pieces of white frit down the centre. The size of the pieces should be no more than $\frac{3}{16}$ inch or you will have difficulty pulling the wire through them.

Lift the brooch carefully with a knife or spatula and place on your wire mesh.

Dry the gum by passing a low flame under the copper. Should you be using a gas and air torch, dry the gum by using a low gas-flame with no air. It is essential that you do not hurry this drying process, otherwise grains of enamel will pop off, resulting in pinpricks in the fired enamel.

Should you be making several brooches you will find that it is only necessary to place the brooch on the warm mesh where it will dry slowly while you prepare other work.

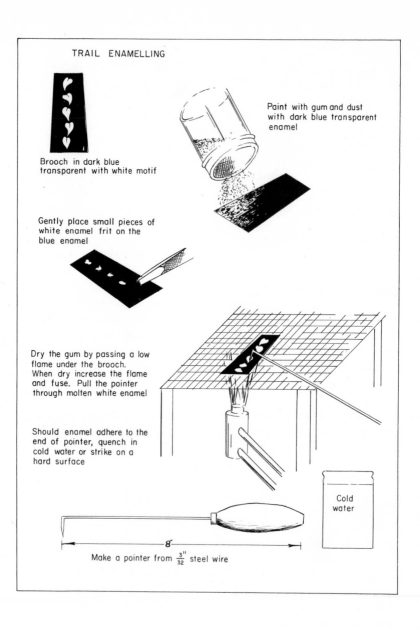

TRAIL ENAMELLING

Brooch in dark blue
transparent with white motif

Paint with gum and dust
with dark blue transparent
enamel

Gently place small pieces of
white enamel frit on the
blue enamel

Dry the gum by passing a low
flame under the brooch.
When dry increase the flame
and fuse. Pull the pointer
through molten white enamel

Should enamel adhere to the
end of pointer, quench in
cold water or strike on a
hard surface

Cold
water

|←———— 8" ————→|

Make a pointer from $\frac{3}{32}$" steel wire

It is possible to check when the gum has dried by looking along the top of the mesh, to make sure that there is no steam rising from the brooch.

To fire the enamel, increase the gas and turn on the air. With a blue flame heat the copper from underneath the mesh. The enamel will turn darker in colour, then to a pebbly surface, and finally to a smooth reflecting surface. When the enamel has reached this stage take your pointer, start at the top and move the point through the pools of white enamel in a wavy motion. Bring your point down the centre and off at the bottom edge. Keep your flame under the brooch to maintain the temperature of the molten enamel while working your design. Make sure that the enamel is fluid and not sticky and pull your pointer along the surface of the enamel rather than cutting through to the metal surface.

Should enamel adhere at your point, tap it on a hard surface or quench in water to remove the enamel.

When trail enamelling, try to complete the piece in one firing, as repeated firing tends to burn out the enamel and give a poor surface.

4   *Planishing an ashtray*

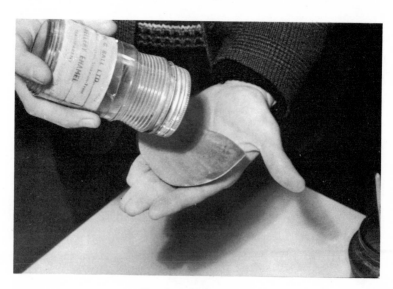

5   *Dusting enamel on ashtray*

6   *Firing ashtray with brazing torch*

7   *Trail-enamelled 5-inch copper ashtrays*

4: Trail-enamelled Ashtray

ASHTRAYS up to 5 inches across can be successfully enamelled on the brazing hearth, and this trailed enamel ashtray shows another variation on decoration by the use of enamel threads.

Cut out your ashtray with a pair of shears, and clean the edges with a file and emery-cloth.

Shape the ashtray on a leather sandbag or a hollowed wood block by using a bossing mallet.

The ashtray can then be annealed by heating to dull red, quenching in water, placing in pickle-bath to remove oxides, and then scrubbing with a brush and pumice-powder until it has a bright appearance with all the oxides removed. Place the ashtray on a stake that fits the shape and planish with a planishing hammer.

Your ashtray is now ready for enamelling and should be degreased and deoxidized.

Hold the ashtray in the palm of your hand and paint the surface with gum.

Dust transparent grey enamel on to the ashtray, starting at the edges and working to the centre. Allow the enamel to fall on the ashtray at right angles by slightly tilting your hand holding the ashtray.

Sprinkle a few coarse pieces of white enamel frit over the grey transparent enamel. Then carefully apply four or five enamel threads down the centre about $\frac{1}{8}$ inch apart.

Place the ashtray on the wire mesh and support it with three pieces of coke or firebrick to prevent it from rocking when working the enamel.

Dry the moisture of the gum and fire as in previous project.

Follow the diagram for the movement of the pointer.

Another alternative design is to make a spiral of $\frac{3}{16}$-inch white enamel frit. Place the pieces about $\frac{1}{4}$ inch to $\frac{3}{8}$ inch apart.

When trailing enamel, start at centre and finish at an edge.

With a little practice you will be able to tell by the colour of the molten enamel when it is ready to be moved with your pointer.

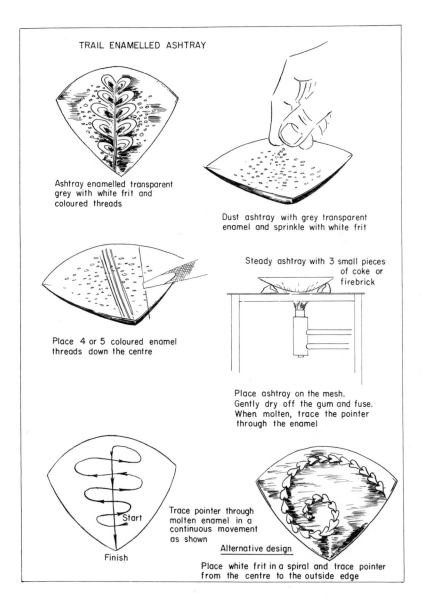

TRAIL ENAMELLED ASHTRAY

Ashtray enamelled transparent grey with white frit and coloured threads

Dust ashtray with grey transparent enamel and sprinkle with white frit

Place 4 or 5 coloured enamel threads down the centre

Steady ashtray with 3 small pieces of coke or firebrick

Place ashtray on the mesh. Gently dry off the gum and fuse. When molten, trace the pointer through the enamel

Start

Finish

Trace pointer through molten enamel in a continuous movement as shown

Alternative design

Place white frit in a spiral and trace pointer from the centre to the outside edge

5: Fish Brooch

Shaping the brooch

WITH a pair of curved hand-shears cut the fish shape out of a piece of 20 SWG copper $2 \times 1\frac{1}{2}$ inches. Clean the edges with a file and emery-cloth.

Place the brooch on a leather sandbag or on a hollowed wood block and shape with a horn mallet.

Prepare the brooch for enamelling as in previous project. Be sure not to touch the copper with your fingers.

Fire a base coat of white enamel and allow the brooch to cool.

When the brooch has cooled remove the oxides from the back by means of the pickle-bath or with emery-cloth. The reason for removing the oxides at each firing stage is to prevent them from contaminating the ground enamel when the next colour is dusted on.

Masking the design

Cut out of paper your shapes for decoration. Coat the white enamelled brooch with gum and place your shapes in position. With your brush, paint the gum over the outside of the paper shapes.

Dust a blue enamel over the entire surface.

With a sharp pointer gently lift the paper mask and remove with a pair of tweezers. The blue enamel will adhere to the gummed paper and leave a clean crisp edge.

Gently dry the moisture of the gum and then fuse the enamel.

Should you use a blue transparent enamel for your second coat you will have a mottled textured surface when fired. This is due to the white enamel, being a softer or lower-firing enamel, bursting through the blue transparent enamel and giving a delightful decorative finish.

Allow the brooch to cool, then remove the oxides from the back and soft solder a brooch pin in position.

Fish brooch 20 S.W.G. Copper blue and white enamel

Cut out fish using shears and beat to shape with horn mallet

Fire a ground coat of white enamel

Cut out paper shapes and a disc for the eye. Dip the shapes in gum and apply to the fish

Paint gum over fish and dust blue enamel evenly

Gently remove paper shapes with tweezers. Paint a small piece of black enamel and place in centre of eye. Dry the gum and fire. Soft solder the pin on the back

6: Sgraffito Ashtray

CUT the ashtray from 20 SWG copper sheet and shape on a leather sandbag or wood block.

The ashtray could then be planished with a hammer and stake.

Prepare the ashtray for enamelling.

Place the ashtray in the palm of your hand, be careful not to touch the inside with your fingers.

Paint the inside surface with gum, taking particular care that the edges are covered.

Dust a black enamel over the entire surface, starting at the edges and working towards the centre. Try to get the grains of enamel falling at 90° to the copper surface. This can be achieved by tilting your hand holding the ashtray.

Allow to dry and then fire.

Allow to cool, then remove the oxides from the back.

Repeat the procedure for dusting enamel, using a light coat of green and tangerine opaque enamel.

Allow the gum to dry and then with a sharp pointer scratch your design through the green enamel frit.

Gently blow the loose particles of enamel from the tray, which will then reveal your design in a black line.

Place your ashtray on a mesh and fire in a kiln or by means of a torch.

The design could be drawn in the moist green enamel and you would obtain a coarse ragged line which is very effective.

When cool remove the oxides and buff the outside copper surface with a calico mop and tripoli compound. Finish with a swansdown mop and rouge.

The copper should then be protected from oxidizing with a clear lacquer.

If no facilities are available for buffing the copper back I have found that fine steel-wool or 'Scotchbrite' abrasive-pad can give a reasonable finish.

Sgraffito ashtray in green and
tangerine opaque enamel

Fire ground coat of black enamel

Paint tray with gum and dust
with green opaque enamel

Lightly dust the edges with
tangerine enamel, then dry gum

When dry scratch design through
green enamel. Gently blow loose
particles of enamel off the tray.
Place tray on mesh and fire

The effect obtained by scratching
the design in wet enamel.
Dry gum before firing

7: *Champlevé Enamel Pendant*

CHAMPLEVÉ enamelling is one of the traditional techniques and comprises a design carved or etched in the surface of the copper or silver. The carved or etched areas are then filled with enamel.

Two methods are suitable for the craft-room; one is the etching of the metal to form the background and cells within the design. The other method is to use two pieces of metal, one for the background, and the other cut out by a piercing saw to form the design. Place the two pieces together and hard solder with enamelling grade.

Plan your design on paper first and shade in the areas that are to be left copper in the finished product. By regarding your design as a stencil you should have no difficulty in the drawing. Remember that the bare copper will contrast with the enamel and arrange the design so that they balance each other and arrive at a harmonious arrangement.

Should your design have an irregular edge or be free form in shape, cut the design out of paper with scissors, place on a piece of 18 SWG copper, and trace round the edge. Use a pair of hand-shears to cut out the copper shape, place in a vice, and clean the edges with a file and emery-cloth.

The design must now be drawn on the copper shape and painted with an acid resistant known as stopping-out varnish. Should the design be a simple or abstract pattern it is only necessary to clean the copper surface and paint the design direct.

Transferring the design

A method of transferring a design to the copper, and one that is successful with children, is by the use of carbon-paper.

Clean the surface of the copper with steel-wool, and, holding the copper by the edges, rinse with water. The copper is clean when the water flows completely off the surface. Should the water form into globules it is an indication that grease is present and further cleaning is required.

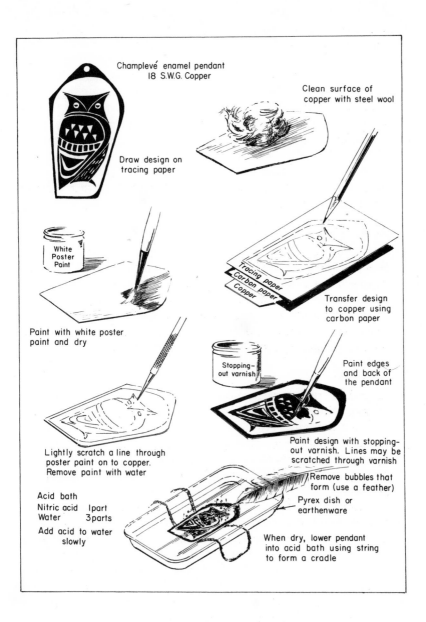

Champlevé enamel pendant
18 S.W.G. Copper

Draw design on
tracing paper

Clean surface of
copper with steel wool

White
Poster
Paint

Tracing paper
Carbon paper
Copper

Transfer design
to copper using
carbon paper

Paint with white poster
paint and dry

Stopping–
out varnish

Paint edges
and back of
the pendant

Lightly scratch a line through
poster paint on to copper.
Remove paint with water

Paint design with stopping-
out varnish. Lines may be
scratched through varnish

Remove bubbles that
form (use a feather)

Acid bath
Nitric acid   1part
Water   3parts
Add acid to water
      slowly

Pyrex dish or
earthenware

When dry, lower pendant
into acid bath using string
to form a cradle

After cleaning, paint the surface with white poster-paint and dry. This gives a good contrast to the carbon line, enabling you to see the design clearly. Take a tracing of your design and with a sharp pencil transfer it to your copper. Using a scriber or similar pointed tool, lightly scratch the design through the poster-paint on to the copper, then remove the paint with water. Dry the copper on a paper towel and avoid touching the surface with your fingers. Place the pendant on a clean sheet of paper and paint the parts of the design that are to remain copper with stopping-out varnish. When dry turn the pendant over and paint the edges and back with the varnish. Take particular care that there are no bare spots or lightly covered areas, and if necessary apply further coats to ensure a perfect resistant surface.

Acid resists

Resists are generally composed of wax, shellac, or asphaltum. Stopping-out varnish consists of asphaltum and beeswax dissolved in benzol or turpentine and this can be purchased from stockists of etching materials.

An easily made resist can be made out of sealing-wax. Crush the sealing-wax into small pieces, place in a small glass jar, cover with methylated spirits, and allow to stand overnight.

Acid-bath

A small 'Pyrex' or earthenware dish is an ideal container for the etching solution. The acid-bath suitable for copper etching consists of 1 part nitric acid to 3 parts water. Pour the **water** into the container **first**, then, wearing rubber gloves, slowly add the acid to the water. Allow about $\frac{1}{2}$ hour for the solution to cool before putting the copper in. Form a cradle with string and lower the pendant into the bath. The bubbles that form with the action of the acid on the copper should be gently brushed away with a feather. Remove the pendant occasionally to check that the resist has not broken down. Should the resist have lifted, rinse the pendant in water, dry, and then coat affected areas with stopping-out varnish, allow to dry and then return the pendant to the bath. Wear rubber gloves to protect your hands when placing the copper in the acid-bath or removing it. When the required depth of $\frac{1}{32}$ inch to $\frac{1}{16}$ inch has been reached remove the pendant and rinse under water.

Remove stopping-out varnish with Turpentine. Drill hole

Turpentine

Shake enamel through 60 mesh sieve

Mix the enamel with Gum Tragacanth

Gum Tragacanth

Pack enamel around the design with spatula and scriber

Cross section through pendant

Before firing

After 1st firing

Repack with enamel

After 2nd firing

Grind enamel level with copper using carborundum stone and water then refire

Lacquer

Remove oxides from copper, using acid or steel wool. Polish on buff and lacquer copper

The stopping-out varnish can be easily removed with turpentine, thinners, or by heating with the torch until all the paint has been completely burnt away. If you burn the varnish off it is only necessary to place the pendant in the pickle-bath and it will be degreased and deoxidized ready for enamelling.

Applying the enamel (wet charging)

Select enamels that have a similar fusion-point to avoid areas burning out through using enamels that have different melting-points.

The enamels most suited are the soft opaques as these contrast very effectively with the polished copper.

Shake the enamel through a 60-mesh sieve on to a clean piece of paper and transfer to a small saucer. Add a few drops of gum tragacanth to the enamel to act as a binder. Using a spatula, pick up a small quantity of enamel and with a scriber pack the enamel into the depressions. Start from the centre of the design and work to the outside; granules of enamel do not then fall on to previously packed areas. Grains of enamel can be removed from the surrounding copper by means of a brush and clean water. A drop of water placed in sharp angular depressions prior to charging with enamel helps to float the enamel grains into the corners. Excess moisture can be removed by placing a corner of blotting-paper on the enamel. Place the pendant on the top of the kiln to dry off the gum prior to firing. Slide a spatula under the pendant and transfer to a wire mesh, place in a preheated kiln and fire.

Finishing the surface

When the pendant has cooled you will notice the enamel has contracted through the particles fusing together. The pendant may be left at this stage if so desired. Genuine champlevé enamelling requires the surface of the enamel to be level with the surrounding copper. This can be achieved by first removing the oxides from the copper by means of the pickle-bath and repacking the cells with enamel and firing once more.

After the second firing it is necessary to grind the surface of the enamel level with the copper. Use a small carborundum-stone with a circular motion to reduce the surface of the enamel. Grind the pendant in a dish of water or place under running water to swill the particles of enamel and carborundum away. When the surface of the pendant is level it requires to be refired to bring back the gloss. If you wish you could leave the enamel a matt finish by not refiring but giving it a polish with pumice-powder and water. After the final firing the oxides should be removed and the copper buffed on the polishing-wheel with tripoli compound and finally polished with rouge on a swansdown mop. In the event of having no mechanical means of polishing the copper, a piece of felt glued on to a piece of flat wood and charged with polishing compound will do just as well, but requires a little extra effort.

Protecting the copper

When the copper has been polished you may if you wish oxidize it by brushing a warm solution of potassium sulphate (liver of sulphur) over the copper surface. Buy the sulphate from the chemist and dissolve a small piece about the size of a hazel-nut in $\frac{1}{4}$ pint of warm water and brush over the pendant. The oxides formed by solution vary from light brown to black. When the desired shade has been reached rinse under water to stop further oxidation and allow to dry.

Whether you oxidize the surface or leave it polished copper, it is necessary to protect it by coating with a clear lacquer. I use 'Johnson's Pellucid Lacquer' which is obtainable from most paint stockists.

It is possible to subject the enamel to a plating bath with no harmful effects should you require the copper silver-plated or gilded.

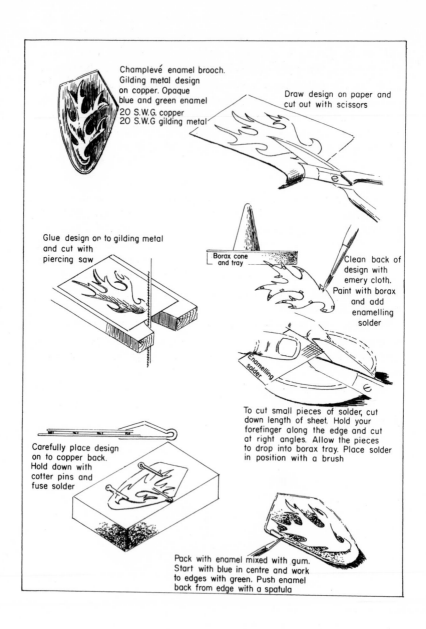

Champlevé enamel brooch. Gilding metal design on copper. Opaque blue and green enamel

20 S.W.G. copper
20 S.W.G gilding metal

Draw design on paper and cut out with scissors

Glue design on to gilding metal and cut with piercing saw

Borax cone and tray

Clean back of design with emery cloth. Paint with borax and add enamelling solder

Enamelling solder

To cut small pieces of solder, cut down length of sheet. Hold your forefinger along the edge and cut at right angles. Allow the pieces to drop into borax tray. Place solder in position with a brush

Carefully place design on to copper back. Hold down with cotter pins and fuse solder

Pack with enamel mixed with gum. Start with blue in centre and work to edges with green. Push enamel back from edge with a spatula

8: Champlevé Enamel Brooch with Gilding Metal Design

In the making of this brooch a piece of 20 SWG copper is used for the background and the design is cut in 20 SWG gilding metal which is then hard soldered to the copper.

Cutting out the motif

Draw the design on paper first and cut out with scissors. Trace round the outside edge on to a piece of copper and cut out with hand-shears. Planish the edge on a stake as in first project to slightly curve the surface. Cut the central motif out of the paper pattern and, using impact adhesive, glue it on to a piece of 20 SWG gilding metal. Place the gilding metal on a vee board and cut out with a piercing saw. Clean the edges with jeweller's files and emery-cloth. Gently tap the motif with a planishing hammer, on the same stake as the one used for the background, to obtain a good joint between the two surfaces.

Hard soldering

Clean the surfaces to be joined with emery-cloth and paint with borax. Place small paillons of enamelling grade solder 800°C, or B6 silver brazing alloy 830°C at each corner and at intervals along the underneath edge of the motif. Carefully place the motif in the centre of the copper and hold in position with cotter-pins as shown. It will keep the pins clear of the edge, and they will hold the two pieces firmly together.

Place the brooch on a charcoal block and heat the whole surface of the brooch with a French blow-torch or brazing torch until the two pieces fuse together. The soldering is completed when a bright line of solder appears round the edge of the motif. On cooling hold the brooch with brass tongs and remove the cotter-pins, then place the brooch in the pickle-bath to remove the borax and oxides.

Enamelling

When the oxides have been removed rinse the brooch in water and place on a paper towel and dry. Transfer the brooch to a clean piece of paper and commence to pack with 100-mesh enamel mixed with gum. Start in the centre with blue opaque enamel and gradually work to the edges with green opaque enamel. Avoid having a hard line between the two enamels by gently blending where they meet with the spatula. Push the enamel back from the edge with the spatula; this helps to protect the edge of the enamel from chipping and forms a copper frame for the enamel.

Dry the moisture off the gum and fire.

The enamel should be left at this stage with only one firing, and the edge and motif cleaned and polished as in previous project.

Soft solder a pin on to the back and protect the bare metal with a coat of lacquer.

8   *Selection of copper pendants*

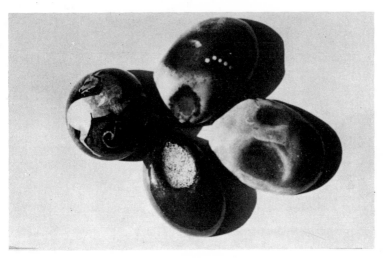

9   *Enamelled copper paperweights*

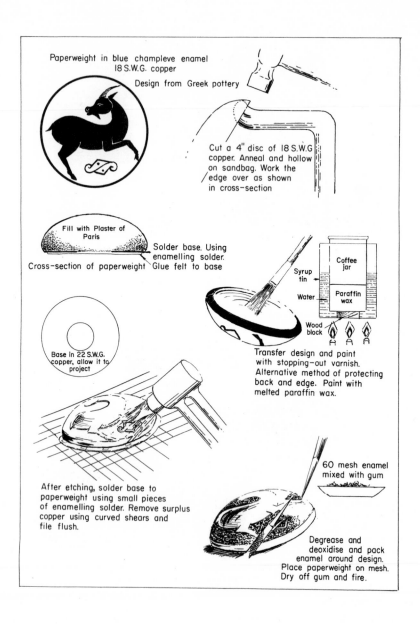

Paperweight in blue champleve enamel
18 S.W.G. copper

Design from Greek pottery

Cut a 4" disc of 18 S.W.G copper. Anneal and hollow on sandbag. Work the edge over as shown in cross-section

Fill with Plaster of Paris

Cross-section of paperweight

Solder base. Using enamelling solder. Glue felt to base

Base in 22 S.W.G. copper, allow it to project

Transfer design and paint with stopping-out varnish. Alternative method of protecting back and edge. Paint with melted paraffin wax.

Coffee jar

Syrup tin

Water

Paraffin wax

Wood block

After etching, solder base to paperweight using small pieces of enamelling solder. Remove surplus copper using curved shears and file flush.

60 mesh enamel mixed with gum

Degrease and deoxidise and pack enamel around design. Place paperweight on mesh. Dry off gum and fire.

9: Champlevé Enamel Paperweight

CUT a disc 4 inches in diameter from a sheet of 18 SWG copper, anneal and shape on a sandbag and stake.

The design should be transferred to the copper surface as in the previous project and then painted with stopping-out varnish.

Use of paraffin wax

An alternative method of protecting the back and edge is by the use of paraffin wax. I have found this suitable in school use and it is easier to remove.

To melt your paraffin wax you require a double boiler similar to a glue-kettle. This can be improvised by placing a coffee-jar on a small piece of wood inside a syrup-tin containing water. Allow the coffee-jar to project past the top of the syrup tin and so prevent water boiling in to the wax.

Use a cheap hog-hair paste-brush to paint the hot wax.

Etch the design in an acid-bath.

When the design has been etched remove the paperweight from the acid-bath by means of brass tongs and rinse under water.

Remove the stopping-out varnish with turpentine or paraffin.

The paraffin wax can be easily removed by placing in hot water or holding under a water-heater and peeling the wax off in a sheet.

Scrub the paperweight with pumice-powder or 'Vim' to remove any trace of wax.

Attaching the base

Cut a base from 22 SWG copper sheet and allow $\frac{1}{4}$ inch in diameter to project round the base of the paperweight. Make a hole in the centre, about $\frac{1}{2}$ inch diameter.

Clean the base and edges to be soldered with emery-cloth and paint with borax. Put the two pieces together on a mesh on the brazing hearth.

Place small pieces of enamelling grade solder at intervals round the edge.

Gently heat the paperweight with the brazing torch to dry off the moisture from the borax. Avoid heating too quickly and causing the borax to bubble and push the pieces of solder away from the edge.

Increase the heat and move the torch over the whole of the surface, heating the paperweight evenly until the solder flows round the edge.

Allow to cool, then remove the oxides in the pickle-bath.

Remove from pickle-bath with brass tongs and rinse in water.

With a pair of curved shears remove the surplus metal round the base. Place flat on the edge of the bench and tidy up the edge with a file and emery-cloth.

Proceed to enamel as in previous project, packing the enamel in the background with a spatula or a pen-nib.

The firing of this project should be carried out in a kiln.

The enamelling may be left at one firing or the areas repacked to bring it level with the surface.

Filling the paperweight

After enamelling and removal of oxides the paperweight should be filled with plaster of paris.

Place a cup of water in a basin and add plaster of paris until it forms a pyramid above the surface of the water; allow to stand for a minute, then stir. The plaster should be a thick creamy consistency which is then poured in the hole in the base.

Gently tap the sides of the paperweight to make the plaster settle and then allow to set.

When the plaster has set the copper design can be polished and lacquered.

Cut a piece of felt and glue to the base with 'Bostik'.

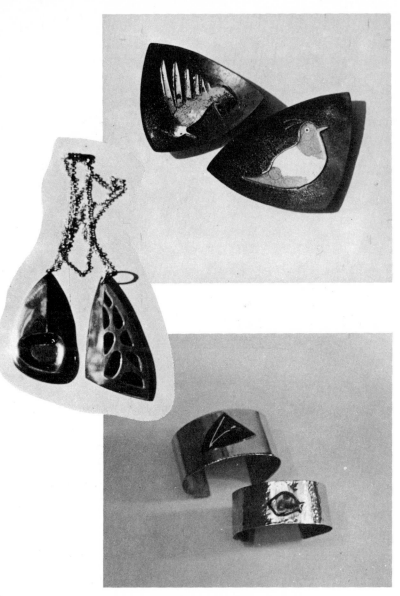

10 *Cloisonné-enamelled ashtrays*

11 *Champlevé-enamelled pendants in copper and gilding metal*

12 *Stainless-steel bracelets with enamel*

Bassetaille enamel
ashtrays. Blue green and
ruby transparent enamel
16 S.W.G. or 18 S.W.G. copper

Stopping-out
varnish

Transfer design to tray
and paint stopping–out
varnish on all areas
painted black. Protect
back and edges with
paraffin wax. Etch
the tray for 1hr to 2hrs.
Remove from acid. Rinse
and dry then paint all
areas cross–hatched and
return to acid bath

Enamel
and gum

Insecticide
spray

Gum diluted
with water

Pack areas
with blue, green and
ruby transparent
enamels

Dilute the gum with water
and lightly spray the tray.
Quickly dust a transparent
enamel over the surface.
Dry off the gum and fire.

10: *Bassetaille Enamel Ashtray*

BASSETAILLE enamelling is similar to champlevé except that transparent enamels are used and cover the whole surface.

By using a two- or three-stage etching technique, packing the background with transparent enamels and then firing a transparent flux over the whole surface, you can obtain a design under enamel giving an illusion of depth.

Cut your ashtray out of 16 SWG or 18 SWG copper, anneal and shape.

Two-stage etching

Transfer the design as previously, or if you are making an abstract design this should be spontaneous and painted direct on to the copper. Protect the back and edges, and place in an acid-bath for about an hour. Remove with brass tongs and rinse under the tap. Dry on a paper towel.

With stopping-out varnish paint further areas of the design. These are shown as shaded portions in the illustration. Allow the varnish to dry completely, then return to the acid-bath for a further period.

Should you be using 16 SWG copper you can repeat this several times. Be careful that you do not etch through the copper, and make sure that you have not disturbed the wax resist on the outside.

In the event of breaking the wax protection you must patch this by painting with wax.

When the ashtray has been etched remove the resists and prepare for enamelling.

Enamelling

Mix 60-mesh enamel with water or gum in a small container and pack the background with transparent coloured enamels and fire.

After firing remove the oxides and scrub with pumice-powder and 'Scotchbrite' abrasive-pad.

Paint the entire surface with gum and dust with a light coat of transparent enamel. Work from the outside edge to the centre.

Should you be enamelling a large area, a light spraying with a mixture of gum and water will prevent the ashtray from drying before you can apply the enamel, and will help to bind the enamel grains.

Allow the ashtray to dry before firing.

An ashtray 5 inches across can be successfully fired on the brazing hearth, but anything larger will require a kiln.

13   *Making enamel threads with a brazing torch*

14   *Collection of enamel threads*

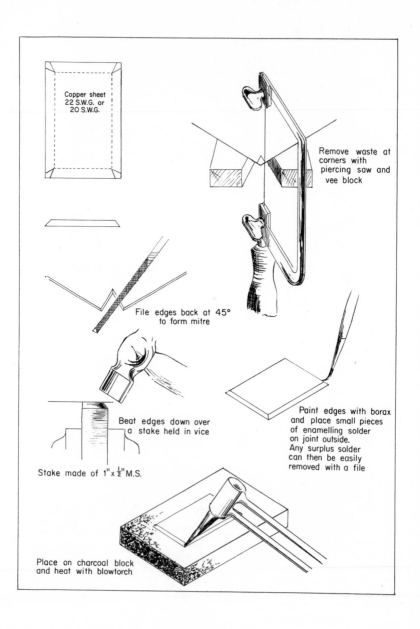

Copper sheet
22 S.W.G. or
20 S.W.G.

Remove waste at
corners with
piercing saw and
vee block

File edges back at 45°
to form mitre

Beat edges down over
a stake held in vice

Stake made of 1" x ½" M.S.

Paint edges with borax
and place small pieces
of enamelling solder
on joint outside.
Any surplus solder
can then be easily
removed with a file

Place on charcoal block
and heat with blowtorch

11: Making a Panel

DECORATIVE enamel panels can be made out of 22 SWG or 24 SWG copper for use on cigarette- and trinket-boxes.

Making panels saves you the problem of having to fire the lid of the box several times, causing warping, and reduces the time necessary to remove the oxides.

Use of a bezel

The panels can be fitted to the lid or sides of the box by means of a bezel. This is a strip of copper or gilding metal hard soldered to the box to form a frame. The enamelled panel is then placed in the frame, which is pushed and worked over the sloping edges setting the panel into position.

The drawings are self-explanatory. Use a sharp scriber and mark out accurately.

Solder the corners with enamelling grade solder.

12: Counter-enamelling

WHEN enamelling a convex surface or a panel that must remain flat it is important that the back is enamelled in addition to the front.

This is known as counter-enamelling and its purpose is to counteract the tension of the front enamel and prevent crazing and warpage.

The principle is the same as veneering a piece of wood. To prevent the board warping both sides should be veneered.

Enamel used for counter-enamelling is the enamel slush that has been collected after washing your enamels.

In the workshop we have a jar for dried slush enamel, also any enamel that has been contaminated with another colour.

The panel should be prepared for enamelling and the back coated with gum and counter-enamel dusted evenly over the surface. Turn the panel over and enamel the face side.

Make supports out of stainless steel and fire in a kiln.

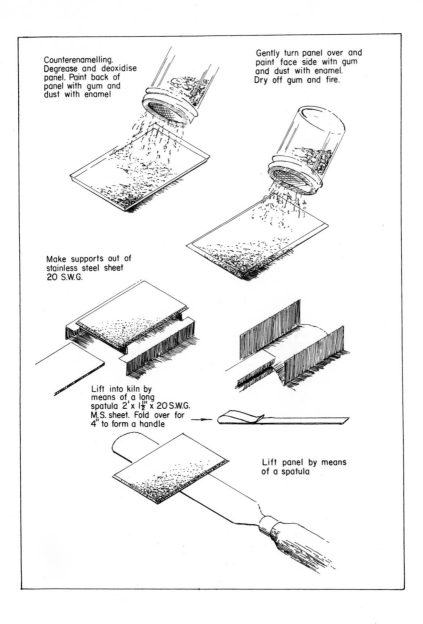

Counterenamelling.
Degrease and deoxidise
panel. Paint back of
panel with gum and
dust with enamel

Gently turn panel over and
paint face side witn gum
and dust with enamel.
Dry off gum and fire.

Make supports out of
stainless steel sheet
20 S.W.G.

Lift into kiln by
means of a long
spatula 2' x 1½" x 20 S.W.G.
M.S. sheet. Fold over for
4" to form a handle

Lift panel by means
of a spatula

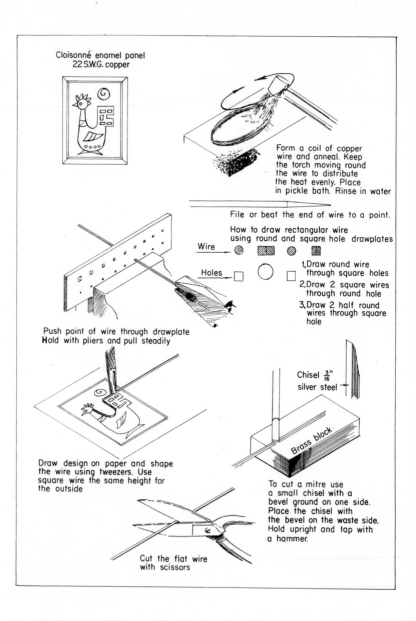

Cloisonné enamel panel
22 S.W.G. copper

Form a coil of copper
wire and anneal. Keep
the torch moving round
the wire to distribute
the heat evenly. Place
in pickle bath. Rinse in water

File or beat the end of wire to a point.

How to draw rectangular wire
using round and square hole drawplates

Wire

Holes

1. Draw round wire
   through square holes
2. Draw 2 square wires
   through round hole
3. Draw 2 half round
   wires through square
   hole

Push point of wire through drawplate
Hold with pliers and pull steadily

Chisel $\frac{3}{16}$"
silver steel

Brass block

Draw design on paper and shape
the wire using tweezers. Use
square wire the same height for
the outside

To cut a mitre use
a small chisel with a
bevel ground on one side.
Place the chisel with
the bevel on the waste side.
Hold upright and tap with
a hammer.

Cut the flat wire
with scissors

68

13: *Cloisonné Enamel Panel, Traditional Method*

CLOISONNÉ enamelling is a traditional technique that requires cloisons or areas partitioned by a wire and then packed with opaque or transparent enamels and fired.

For this project it is necessary to draw your design to size on a drawing paper.

Make a panel from 22 SWG copper by following the instructions on making a panel.

The drawing of wire

The wire ribbon should be made from 24 SWG copper wire which is annealed and passed through metal rollers.

Should you have no metal rollers, you will have to flatten the wire on a stake with a planishing hammer, or follow the diagram for drawing wire through drawplates. The size of the wire should be between $\frac{1}{32}$ inch and $\frac{1}{16} \times \cdot 012$ inch in thickness (about the thickness of a cigarette-packet).

Building the design

Shape the design with the ribbon by working on top of the drawing and bending the ribbon with tweezers. The wire can be easily cut with scissors. The outside wire forming the frame should be formed out of square wire and be of the same depth as the ribbon. Mitres are formed by cutting with a sharp chisel on a brass block. To ensure a clean upright cut, the chisel should be ground on one side only.

Hard soldering the wires

When the wires have been formed the panel requires scrubbing with pumice-powder to remove any grease. Avoid handling the surface as this tends to prevent the solder from flowing.

Heat each piece of the design and quench in a pickle-bath, rinse in water, and place on a paper towel to dry.

Hold each piece of the design with tweezers, paint the edge with borax, and place in position.

Place paillons of enamelling grade solder at each joint and one or two along the edges.

Lift the panel with a knife and place on a mesh.

Gently heat the panel to remove the moisture from the borax. Increase the flame and fuse into position.

When cool place the panel in the pickle-bath to remove the oxides and rinse in water.

Enamelling

Proceed to pack enamel in the cloisons by means of a pen-nib or spatula. Start in the centre, filling the small areas first and working to the outside edge. This prevents any grains of enamel falling on previously packed areas.

Dry off the moisture and fire.

Traditional cloisonné enamel is level with wires, and it will be necessary to repack the areas after the first firing.

The enamel and wires are then ground flat by using carborundum-stones, using a circular motion and grinding under water.

When level the enamel is brought back to a glossy finish by refiring.

The oxides are then removed from the wires by placing the panel in the pickle-bath.

The panel is now ready for mounting in a bezel.

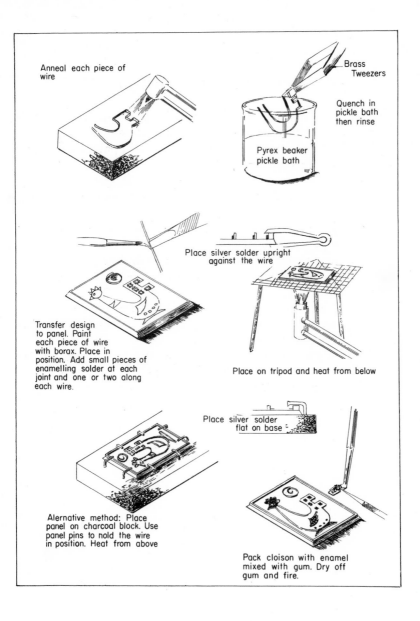

Anneal each piece of wire

Brass Tweezers

Quench in pickle bath then rinse

Pyrex beaker pickle bath

Place silver solder upright against the wire

Transfer design to panel. Paint each piece of wire with borax. Place in position. Add small pieces of enamelling solder at each joint and one or two along each wire.

Place on tripod and heat from below

Place silver solder flat on base

Alernative method: Place panel on charcoal block. Use panel pins to nold the wire in position. Heat from above

Pack cloison with enamel mixed with gum. Dry off gum and fire.

14: Cloisonné Pendant, Simplified Method

SHAPE your pendant from 20 SWG copper sheet, place it on a piece of drawing paper and draw round it. Draw a design to fit the shape. With this method you must have at least one curve or bend in your wire to allow it to be free-standing.

Prepare the wire as in previous project and shape with tweezers.

Enamel the pendant with a light coat of transparent flux and allow to cool.

Hold each piece of wire with tweezers, paint the edge with gum, and place on the fired enamel.

Transfer the pendant to a mesh, gently dry the gum, and fire. The wires will settle into the molten enamel and be held firm when cool.

Should any wires not completely settle into the enamel it is possible to push them down with a metal rod when using fire-enamelling technique.

When using a kiln, should any wires not have fused, quickly press a spatula on the top before the enamel has time to cool.

The design can then be packed with enamels or left at this stage.

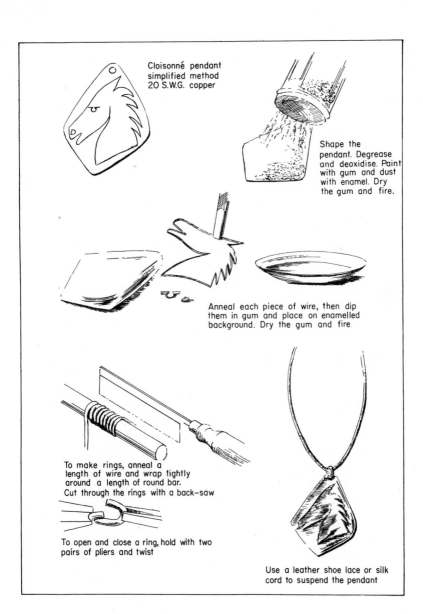

Cloisonné pendant
simplified method
20 S.W.G. copper

Shape the
pendant. Degrease
and deoxidise. Paint
with gum and dust
with enamel. Dry
the gum and fire.

Anneal each piece of wire, then dip
them in gum and place on enamelled
background. Dry the gum and fire.

To make rings, anneal a
length of wire and wrap tightly
around a length of round bar.
Cut through the rings with a back-saw

To open and close a ring, hold with two
pairs of pliers and twist

Use a leather shoe lace or silk
cord to suspend the pendant

15: Repoussé Work

REPOUSSÉ work is normally worked on pitch held in a heavy cast-iron bowl that can be rotated in a leather or rope ring. An alternative method is with the pitch held in a wood tray.

A small bowl can be successfully made from an old copper ball that can be found in plumbers' workshops and scrapyards.

Weight the ball by half-filling with lead.

Make the ring from $1 \times \frac{1}{4}$ inch leather and join the ends together by means of a small piece of leather drilled and bolted on the outside of the joint.

Pitch

Make the pitch compound by first weighing out your ingredients (see page 76). Place the pitch in an old pan and slowly melt on a gas-ring. When the pitch has melted, stir in the plaster of paris and add the resin and tallow. When the ingredients are completely mixed together pour into the bowl or wood tray and allow to cool.

This is a basic pitch formula that I have used and have found suitable. However, temperature conditions vary; should you find the compound too brittle add tallow, if too soft add pitch.

Small work can be worked on thick lino, sheet lead, or on the end grain of a wood block, provided that no heavy relief-work is required.

The metal blank is placed on the wood block and nails are driven in round the edge and then hammered over.

Tools

Repoussé tools are in three categories: tracing tools, bossing tools, and matting tools.

The tracing tools are used for chasing the outline of the design.

Bossing tools are used for modelling, and punching the form out, working on the underneath side.

Matting tools are used generally to texture the background. The work is supported on a hard surface and the background punched flat.

The tools can be purchased or they can be made out of $\frac{3}{16}$ inch or $\frac{1}{4}$ inch square or round silver steel about 4 inches in length. I prefer the square steel for making tracing tools as they are easier to handle and have less likelihood of twisting in your fingers.

Tracing tools have a blunt edge and I prefer a slight radius on the length of the edge to facilitate the tilting back of the tool when using.

Bossing tools may be square, round, or rectangular; these can be filed or turned and must have no sharp edges.

Matting tools can be made by sawing, filing, or punching the working end before hardening.

All the tools must be cleaned and polished and then hardened and tempered to medium straw colour.

Leaf-shaped brooch

To make the leaf you should draw the design direct on the copper sheet or cut the shape out of paper and glue it down on the copper.

The leaf shape is then cut out on a vee block with a piercing saw, annealed by heating to dull red, and quenched in water. Remove the oxides in the pickle-bath. Gently heat the pitch with a low gas-flame; do not overheat and allow the pitch to bubble as this causes it to lose its adhesive qualities and form air-pockets.

Place the leaf face-side-up on the softened pitch and allow to set.

Hold the tracer in your fingers as shown in the illustration. Make sure you hold the tracer firmly and tilt the tool away from you. The tool should then be struck rhythmically with the repoussé hammer, causing the tool to move forward slowly, cutting a continuous groove. This action requires a little practice until you find the correct angle to hold the tool. I find that a spot of oil on the cutting edge helps to allow the tracer to slide forward.

When all the veins have been traced remove the leaf from the pitch block by inserting the tracing tool under an edge and prising upwards.

The pitch should now be removed from the back of the leaf by heating with the brazing torch until it turns to ash. This burning off the ash also anneals the copper for the next stage.

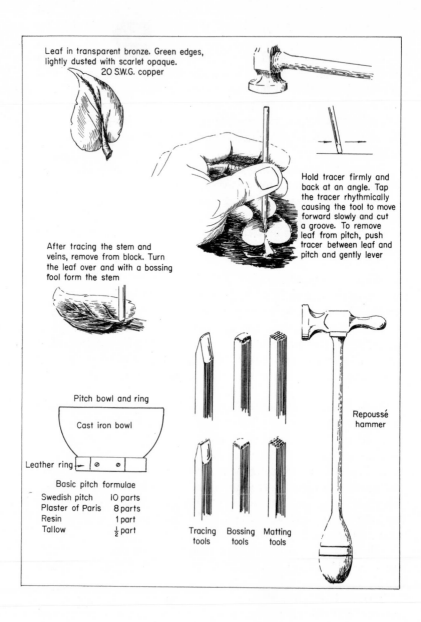

Leaf in transparent bronze. Green edges, lightly dusted with scarlet opaque. 20 S.W.G. copper

Hold tracer firmly and back at an angle. Tap the tracer rhythmically causing the tool to move forward slowly and cut a groove. To remove leaf from pitch, push tracer between leaf and pitch and gently lever

After tracing the stem and veins, remove from block. Turn the leaf over and with a bossing fool form the stem

Pitch bowl and ring

Cast iron bowl

Leather ring

Basic pitch formulae

Swedish pitch	10 parts
Plaster of Paris	8 parts
Resin	1 part
Tallow	$\frac{1}{2}$ part

Tracing tools

Bossing tools

Matting tools

Repoussé hammer

Remove the oxides that have formed on the copper leaf and place the leaf face-down on the softened pitch. With a bossing tool model the forms by tapping down in between the veins, and form the stem.

The leaf should now be removed from the pitch with your tracing tool and the pitch removed from the face-side.

Prepare the leaf for enamelling. Dust a transparent green over the surface and lightly tip the edges with a scarlet opaque enamel.

Dry the enamel and then fire.

Soft solder a pin on to the back.

16: Painted Enamel Brooch in a Bezel Setting

IN traditional Limoges enamelling the design is built up stage by stage with fine-ground opaque and transparent enamels and fired on to a white or copper background. The panels are worked over evenly, with the enamel being brought up to the same thickness throughout the panel, and requiring several firings.

Preparation and firing of overglaze enamel

Enamel can be prepared for painting by grinding to a fine powder with a mortar and pestle and then grinding to infinity with a ground-glass slab and muller. A few drops of lavender oil or oil of cloves are added to act as a binder.

However, today there are available enamels known as overglaze enamels; these consist of fine-ground enamels and can be purchased with or without flux. The enamels without flux require a soft fusing flux to be dusted over the surface on the final firing.

The enamels that we use in school are the former and require no added flux.

They can be purchased in small quantities such as 1-ounce packets. These should be stored in small glass jars or phials to prevent them deteriorating with the atmosphere.

Overglaze enamels are very delicate; they have a firing range of 700° C and must be fired carefully in a muffle.

I have found that the small hot-plate type of kiln is suitable for this type of work, as you can watch the enamel and remove it quickly as soon as it has fired. Should you have no kiln and rely on the fire-enamelling technique, it will be necessary to make a muffle from a strip of stainless steel about 9 inches × 3 inches, which should be bent to form a 3-inch × 1¼-inch rectangle.

This should be placed on the mesh, and the brooch placed inside to protect it from the flame. Keep an eye on the fusion of the enamel and remove as soon as it has become glossy.

To prepare your panel you should cut an ellipse from 24 SWG

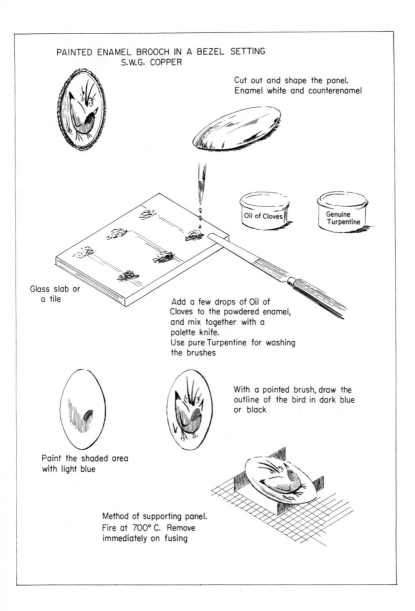

PAINTED ENAMEL BROOCH IN A BEZEL SETTING
S.W.G. COPPER

Cut out and shape the panel.
Enamel white and counterenamel

Oil of Cloves

Genuine
Turpentine

Glass slab or
a tile

Add a few drops of Oil of
Cloves to the powdered enamel,
and mix together with a
palette knife.
Use pure Turpentine for washing
the brushes

With a pointed brush, draw the
outline of the bird in dark blue
or black

Paint the shaded area
with light blue

Method of supporting panel.
Fire at 700° C. Remove
immediately on fusing

copper sheet and shape on a hollow block with a horn mallet, or run round the edge with a doming tool or ball-peen hammer.

Prepare the copper for enamelling and counter-enamelling as in previous project and enamel the face-side white.

Method of painting

Place a small quantity of enamel on a glass slab or tile, add a few drops of lavender oil or oil of cloves and mix together with a palette knife.

The medium sold by enamel suppliers for binding the enamel is known as 'Fat Oil'.

Use genuine turpentine, not turpentine substitute, for washing your brushes and thinning your enamel paint.

There are various techniques for overglaze enamelling; you can lay paints next to one another, they can be stippled, several colours can be marbled together, you can draw in the paint with your finger, a matt background can be achieved by dabbing with cotton-wool covered in a fine cloth.

With the bird design I have tried to illustrate how a motif can be achieved with very few brush-strokes and how the brush-marks can give it a spontaneous look. There are several designs at the rear of the book following a similar pattern. Practise them on a tile until you can get the feel of using a brush freely.

Should you make a mistake it is only necessary to remove the paint with a cloth and a drop of turpentine.

Ideally you should leave the enamel to dry slowly for several hours to allow the oil to evaporate. This can be hastened by placing at the mouth of the kiln for a second or two and withdrawing. Repeat this action until the oil has completely burnt away.

When all trace of smoke has gone, place in your muffle and fire at 700° C (a dull red) for approximately 1 minute. Check the fusion at your peephole and remove immediately it has fired. Should you leave it longer the white enamel background will begin to craze. In the event of this happening you should allow the panel to remain in the kiln until the enamel fuses together.

Some colours tend to burn out even at 700° C, and it will be necessary to paint over them and build a heavier coat.

Decorative scenes can be painted, and these are achieved by building up the depth of colour with several firings.

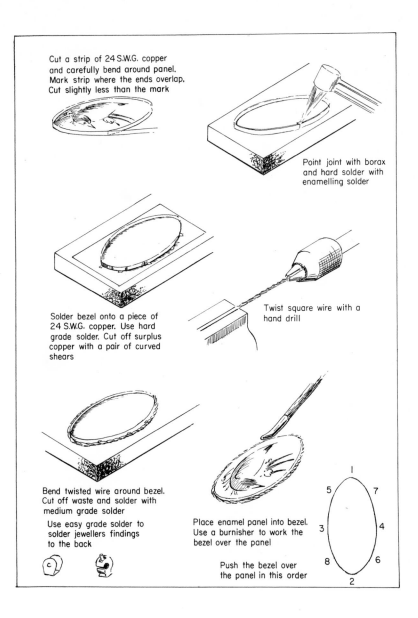

Cut a strip of 24 S.W.G. copper
and carefully bend around panel.
Mark strip where the ends overlap.
Cut slightly less than the mark

Point joint with borax
and hard solder with
enamelling solder

Solder bezel onto a piece of
24 S.W.G. copper. Use hard
grade solder. Cut off surplus
copper with a pair of curved
shears

Twist square wire with a
hand drill

Bend twisted wire around bezel.
Cut off waste and solder with
medium grade solder

Use easy grade solder to
solder jewellers findings
to the back

Place enamel panel into bezel.
Use a burnisher to work the
bezel over the panel

Push the bezel over
the panel in this order

81

Making the bezel setting

After the decoration of the panel it must be mounted in a bezel. This is one of the methods of use when working in precious metals when you require jewellers' finding to be hard soldered to the back. The same method is also used for mounting panels to trinket-boxes, etc., when you cannot fire the whole box (see also page 65).

The diagrams are self-explanatory. Use the different grades of silver solder, starting with the highest melting-point enamelling solder 800° C, to easy grade solder 700° C, to build up the setting. Complete the setting and oxidize the copper with liver of sulphur to give it an antique finish if you wish. The enamel is then placed in the setting and the bezel pushed over with a burnisher, working at alternate ends as in the diagram and finally rubbing down to a close fit on the panel.

17: Lustres

LUSTRES are metallic compounds that are suspended in volatile oils. Gold, silver, platinum, and coloured lustres are supplied in a liquid state ready for use. Also available are reducing media for the thinning of lustres and washing brushes.

Liquid gold is used as an overglaze decoration and should be used on the last and separate firings.

The use of lustres

When using a combination of overglaze enamels and lustres complete the painting in enamel and fire, then add your lustre. The reason for a separate firing is that the lustres do not mix with turpentine. Any brushes and pens used must be kept separate.

Fine lines of liquid gold can be applied by means of fine-pointed sable-hair brushes or with a mapping-pen.

Take the utmost care when using lustres, as finger-marks will result in firing a purple colour. Should you make a mistake remove with thinners and rub vigorously with saliva.

Firing

Before firing, the oils should be allowed to dissipate, as with the overglaze enamels. However, this can be speeded up by placing at the mouth of the kiln for a minute or two until there is no trace of smoke.

The enamel should then be placed in the kiln and fired at 700° C for approximately 1 minute.

If the liquid gold rubs off when fired, then the enamel was underfired and will require repainting and refiring. Overfiring tends to cause the lustres to become dull.

Should you use lustres with children in the school workshop I recommend that the small bottles are placed in holes drilled in a block of wood to prevent them from being spilled and the brushes and pens kept in a separate container.

Use lustres with restraint; a little gold goes a long way.

18: Making Enamel Threads and Eyes

ENAMEL threads are made by placing enamel frit into a crucible or a piece of hollowed mild steel or copper sheet.

Place the crucible on a brazing hearth and pack small pieces of coke round it. Play your torch on the side, directing the flame downwards until the heat begins to fuse the enamel. When the enamel begins to fuse bring your torch up and direct your flame on top of the enamel. On the enamel reaching molten stage dip a $\frac{1}{8}$-inch steel rod into it and withdraw, pulling out a thread of enamel. Cut the thread at the crucible by means of the torch-flame, then cut from the steel rod, and allow the thread to drop on a table or the floor. These coloured threads of enamel are easy to make and I find that children enjoy making them.

For those who have no brazing hearth and are using a 'Calor' gas-torch, a simple hearth can be made out of a biscuit-tin by cutting one side off and having three sides about 4 inches in depth. This will support your coke and crucible and prevent the coke from falling on the table or bench.

Enamel beads or eyes are easily made by placing small pieces of enamel frit on to a charcoal block or firebrick and gently heating with a French blow-torch or a small tip on a gas-torch. The pieces of frit will form a globule and by means of a coloured enamel thread contrasting colours can be added.

Should you require several similar size beads take a thread of enamel and with a pair of tweezers break into small equal lengths. These should then be placed on the charcoal block and formed into beads with the torch.

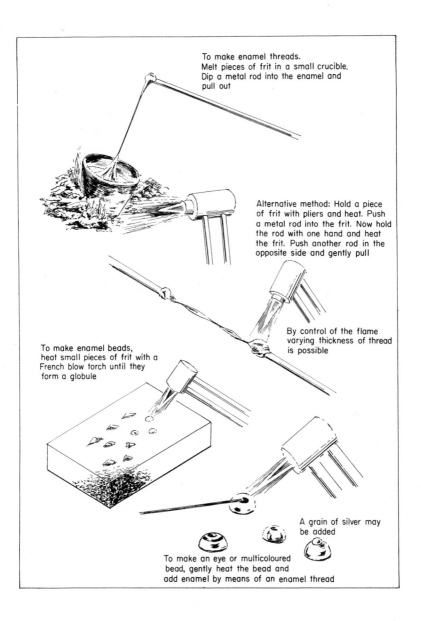

To make enamel threads.
Melt pieces of frit in a small crucible.
Dip a metal rod into the enamel and
pull out

Alternative method: Hold a piece
of frit with pliers and heat. Push
a metal rod into the frit. Now hold
the rod with one hand and heat
the frit. Push another rod in the
opposite side and gently pull

By control of the flame
varying thickness of thread
is possible

To make enamel beads,
heat small pieces of frit with a
French blow torch until they
form a globule

A grain of silver may
be added

To make an eye or multicoloured
bead, gently heat the bead and
add enamel by means of an enamel thread

19: *Additional Techniques in Enamel*

Use of stencils

STENCILS can be cut from thin card or paper for use in the decorating of enamel. Interesting effects can be obtained by the use of various mesh hair-nets, doilies, and natural shapes such as leaves and grasses.

Producing a line in enamel

Lines can be drawn in the enamel prior to firing (sgraffito). They can be drawn with a brush or pen with gum and dusted with enamel. Threads or string can be dipped in screening enamel or slip enamel and laid on to the enamel surface. The thread is then gently removed, leaving an imprint of enamel. Steel enamel can be slip-trailed similar to trailing a glaze in pottery. Straight and curved lines can be made with enamel threads fired on to the enamel.

Creating textures

By deliberately underfiring enamel you will acquire a pebbly surface. If you overfire a transparent enamel that has been dusted on an opaque enamel you will have a mottled finish due to the soft opaque enamel fusing before the transparent enamel and breaking through the surface.

Crushed glass and beads can be fused in the enamel surface but should be used with restraint or they will craze and break off.

Interesting effects can be obtained by fusing strands of fibreglass on enamel.

A scintillating effect can be obtained by firing transparent enamels over granules of silver or mica. Silver and copper filings can be sprinkled on the surface and allowed to fuse into the enamel.

Building plant forms

Unusual forms can be made by placing one or two enamel threads on a charcoal block and gently heating with a small torch, bending the threads to shape. Small pieces of enamel frit can be added to give a seaweed effect.

Use of firescale

By firing flux over oxides you will obtain an unusual enamel background. With normal enamelling procedure the firescale or oxides are removed by the pickle-bath.

Deliberately form a heavy firescale on the copper surface by heating the copper bright red and keeping it at this temperature for a minute or two. Do not place in the pickle-bath, but allow to cool slowly. The firescale will form interesting shapes if placed in cold water before it is entirely cool, or it can be partly removed by emery-cloth to form an abstract shape.

Flux or transparent amber and greys give an interesting colour range, depending on the deposit of firescale.

20: Bracelet in Stainless Steel, Nickel Silver, or Copper with Enamel

SHOULD you make the bracelet out of stainless steel or nickel silver the gauge of metal should be 22 SWG. If the bracelet is made from copper 20 SWG is suitable.

The size of the bracelet will vary according to size of wrist. The size given in the diagram is for an average adult. Check the size of the wrist that you wish the bracelet to fit by means of a strip of paper and alter the width to correspond if necessary.

Mark out the bracelet size accurately on the metal sheet and cut out with hand-shears. Place in a vice or support on the edge of the bench and clean the edges with a file and emery-cloth. Anneal the copper by heating to dull red and quenching in water. The oxides should now be removed in the pickle-bath and scrubbed, or with emery-cloth. The bracelet can now be given a decorative surface by planishing, or left plain, and the edges worked with a planishing hammer or collet hammer.

To shape the bracelet bend round a mandril, or if no mandril is available a milk-bottle would suffice.

The copper motif should now be cut from 22 SWG copper sheet and curved on the mandril to fit the curve of the bracelet.

Enamel the motif, clean the oxides from the back, and tin the surface with soft solder. Place the motif in position on the bracelet and heat from below until the solder flows round the edge.

BRACELET IN STAINLESS STEEL, NICKEL STEEL OR COPPER WITH ENAMEL MOTIF

Cut motif from 22 S.W.G. copper and shape to curve of bracelet.
Enamel in dark colours, add wire or threads of enamel

Pattern of bracelet.
Cut from stainless steel etc.

← 6" →

Edge decoration can be made with a collet hammer and stake

Form bracelet shape with a mallet

Soft solder motif onto bracelet

89

21: Three-Dimensional Wall Panels

THESE panels are ideal projects for pupils, giving them plenty of scope for their imagination and free expression. Their charm derives from the simplicity of the design, and the contrast between the colourful enamels and the natural wood.

Panel with fish motif

The fish are made similar to the previous project of a fish brooch and the sea vegetation is cut freely from 20 SWG copper sheet.

There are many illustrations of sea life to stir the imagination and you could use your own initiative and design your own panel.

The panel in this project is made from $\frac{5}{8}$-inch oak in a natural wax finish. The board is chamfered at the edges with a plane and sand-papered perfectly smooth, finishing with Grade 0 and working with the grain of the wood.

Coat the board with white or extra pale shellac polish that has been diluted with methylated spirits. Do this quickly, making sure that you have covered the entire surface and edges, and with a cloth wipe the surplus off and allow to dry.

The surface is then worked over with 00 steel-wool and furniture-wax until smooth, and then it is rubbed vigorously with a soft cloth. When the fish and sea vegetation have been enamelled the oxides are removed from the back and round-headed copper slate nails are soft soldered in position. The nails should be cut to vary the projection of the motifs and give an illusion of depth. The supports could be made by hard soldering $\frac{1}{8}$-inch brazing rod into $\frac{1}{8}$-inch brass washers or by turning on a lathe from $\frac{5}{16}$-inch brass rod.

Place your fish on the panel, mark their position, and drill the holes with a $\frac{1}{8}$-inch drill, being careful not to drill through the panel.

The enamels are then glued into position with 'Araldite' or 'Bostik' adhesive.

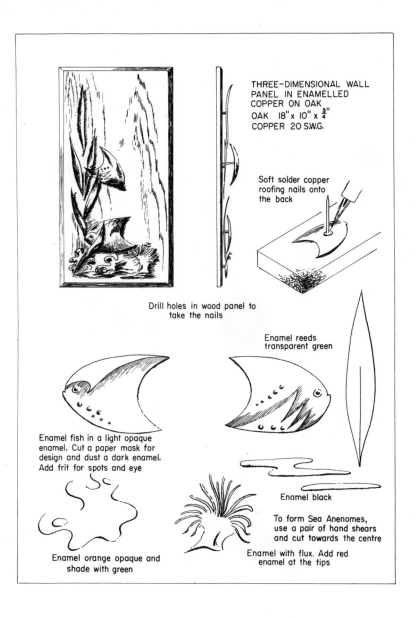

THREE-DIMENSIONAL WALL
PANEL IN ENAMELLED
COPPER ON OAK
OAK 18" x 10" x $\frac{3}{4}$"
COPPER 20 S.W.G.

Soft solder copper
roofing nails onto
the back

Drill holes in wood panel to
take the nails

Enamel reeds
transparent green

Enamel fish in a light opaque
enamel. Cut a paper mask for
design and dust a dark enamel.
Add frit for spots and eye

Enamel black

To form Sea Anenomes,
use a pair of hand shears
and cut towards the centre

Enamel with flux. Add red
enamel at the tips

Enamel orange opaque and
shade with green

91

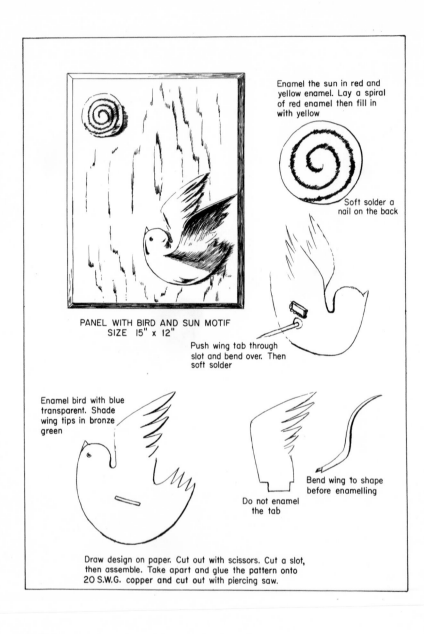

Enamel the sun in red and yellow enamel. Lay a spiral of red enamel then fill in with yellow

Soft solder a nail on the back

PANEL WITH BIRD AND SUN MOTIF
SIZE 15" x 12"

Push wing tab through slot and bend over. Then soft solder

Enamel bird with blue transparent. Shade wing tips in bronze green

Do not enamel the tab

Bend wing to shape before enamelling

Draw design on paper. Cut out with scissors. Cut a slot, then assemble. Take apart and glue the pattern onto 20 S.W.G. copper and cut out with piercing saw.

Panel with bird and sun motif

The bird design could be made in thin card first and then transferred to 20 SWG copper sheet and cut out with hand-shears and piercing saw.

Bend the projecting wing to shape before enamelling and protect the tab from the enamel by masking with a strip of paper.

After the bird and wing have been enamelled remove the oxides from the back.

Push the tab of the projecting wing through the slot and bend over and soft solder in position.

Soft solder copper nails to the back of the sun and bird motifs and attach to the board as in previous project.

Wall panel with duck motif

The making of this panel is similar to the previous projects.

The ducks can be enamelled in one colour to form a silhouette or they could be enamelled white and then painted in natural colours by means of overglaze enamels.

WALL PANEL WITH DUCK MOTIF

Draw out design on paper and proceed
as in previous project

Shape wing
before enamelling

Enamel ducks in
transparent green or
in natural colours,
using overglaze
colours on white

Enamel hills dark blue. Place small hill behind large hill

Soft solder wing tabs and
copper roofing nails to the back

94

15 & 16 *Three-dimensional wall panels, wood with enamelled copper*

22: Mosaic Fish

THIS design shows how it is possible to make large decorative enamels that can be mounted on large panels of plywood or used individually as wall decorations. The fish is cut out of 20 SWG copper sheet with a pair of hand-shears and the edges cleaned with a file.

Trace round the copper shape on to $\frac{1}{4}$-inch plywood and cut out with a coping saw.

Cut the copper shape into sections and enamel in contrasting colours. The tails and fins are made from 20 SWG and 24 SWG copper wire.

Shape the wires and place them on a charcoal block.

Paint each joint with 'Fryolux' solder, paint and gently heat with a torch. The projecting fin should be made from $\frac{1}{16}$-inch brazing rod, and the two pieces hard soldered together. This fin should then be polished with steel-wool and lacquered.

After building the tail and fins paint with a matt black paint.

Mark the position for the fins on the edge of the plywood shape and drill holes to receive the wire. Paint the plywood shape matt black and allow to dry. Glue the fins and enamelled pieces into position with impact adhesive.

Variation on mosaic: beetle and grasshopper

These projects show a variation on the use of mosaic enamel. They can be mounted on to wood panels by soft soldering nails to the back, or a keyhole can be made from a strip of copper which is then soft soldered into position.

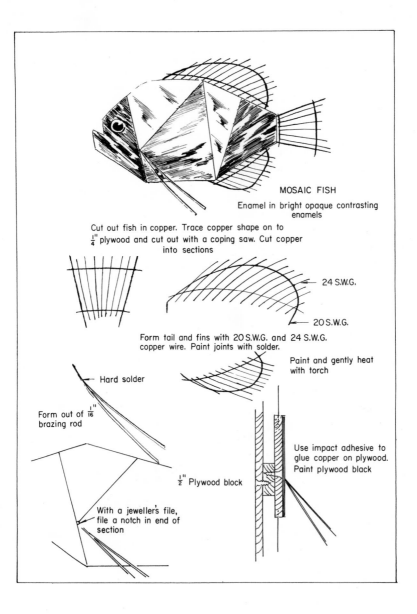

MOSAIC FISH

Enamel in bright opaque contrasting enamels

Cut out fish in copper. Trace copper shape on to $\frac{1}{4}$" plywood and cut out with a coping saw. Cut copper into sections

← 24 S.W.G.

← 20 S.W.G.

Form tail and fins with 20 S.W.G. and 24 S.W.G. copper wire. Paint joints with solder.

Paint and gently heat with torch

← Hard solder

Form out of $\frac{1}{16}$" brazing rod

$\frac{1}{2}$" Plywood block

Use impact adhesive to glue copper on plywood. Paint plywood black

With a jeweller's file, file a notch in end of section

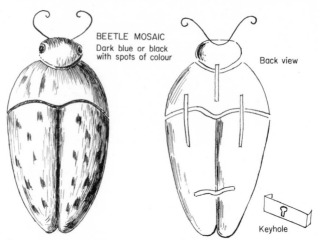

BEETLE MOSAIC
Dark blue or black
with spots of colour

Back view

Keyhole

Cut out shapes from 22 S.W.G. copper and shape with a mallet on sandbag. Counter enamel the back. Place strips of paper on portion to be soldered. Build sections with $\frac{1}{16}$" or $\frac{1}{8}$" brazing rod. Soft solder. For individual hanging cut a keyhole in a strip of copper and soft solder to the back

GRASSHOPPER MOSAIC
Enamel green with brass legs

Soft solder nails onto back

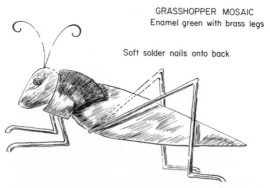

Cut out the three sections. Shape the legs out of $\frac{1}{8}$" brazing rod, the back legs in one piece and the front legs in one piece. Shape the antennae out of 22 S.W.G. copper wire. Soft solder legs and antennae onto the back.

98

17   *Mosaic fish panel, enamelled copper*

18   *Mosaic fish in steel, length 24 inches*

99

23: Wrought-Iron Cross with Enamel Inlay

BY using enamel with wrought iron and mild steel you have a combination of strength and colour. The brilliance of the enamels contrasts with the steel, giving highlights and accents of colour to what is normally a rather dull material.

Draw the cross accurately on a sheet of mild steel and make the two pieces out of $\frac{5}{16}$-inch square mild steel bar.

The corners are made by marking the bar from the master drawing and a mitre is cut partially through the bar. Heat this section of bar and bend on the anvil, or by holding at the mitre with a pair of flat forge tongs. After bending ensure that it has not twisted, and quench in water.

Proceed to bend the next mitre. The corners can be strengthened by brazing, or hard soldering with 'Easy Flo'.

Place the cross-piece on the upright and mark the position of the four halving joints.

Hard solder $\frac{1}{8}$-inch M.S. rods in between to wire the enamels to.

Clean up with a file and give two coats of matt black paint.

Make a template for your enamels out of thin card, transfer the shape to 20 SWG copper and cut with a pair of shears.

The copper surface can then be embellished with the planishing hammer or repoussé tools or left plain. Enamel the pieces of copper and clean the back. Mark the position for wires from the cross. Soft solder the copper wires to the back of the enamels.

Place the five triangular enamels in position and twist the copper wire round the $\frac{1}{8}$-inch M.S. rods. Cut off the surplus wire with a pair of pliers.

The base consists of a piece of 7-inch × 3-inch oak 12 inches in length. Mark the centre and cut a mortise to fit the cross.

The base is finished natural and waxed.

Use 'Araldite' to glue the cross in the base.

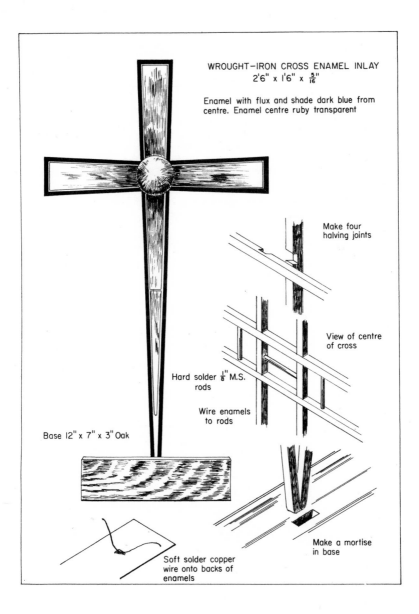

WROUGHT—IRON CROSS ENAMEL INLAY
2'6" x 1'6" x $\frac{5}{16}$"

Enamel with flux and shade dark blue from centre. Enamel centre ruby transparent

Make four halving joints

View of centre of cross

Hard solder $\frac{1}{8}$" M.S. rods

Wire enamels to rods

Base 12" x 7" x 3" Oak

Make a mortise in base

Soft solder copper wire onto backs of enamels

19 *Cross in gilding metal and blue-enamelled copper, height 2 feet*

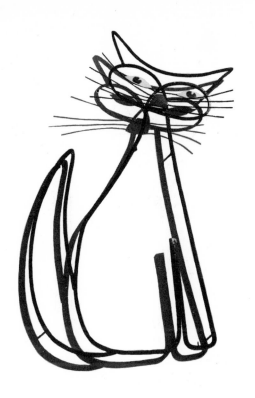

20 & 21   *Wall decorations in wrought iron and enamel; cat and gull*

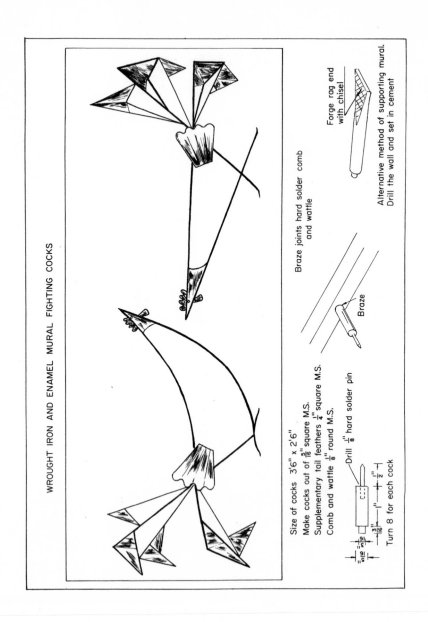

WROUGHT IRON AND ENAMEL MURAL FIGHTING COCKS

Braze joints hard solder comb and wattle

Forge rag end with chisel

Alternative method of supporting mural. Drill the wall and set in cement

Braze

Size of cocks 3'6" x 2'6"
Make cocks out of $\frac{5}{16}$" square M.S.
Supplementary tail feathers $\frac{1}{4}$" square M.S.
Comb and wattle $\frac{1}{8}$" round M.S.

Drill $\frac{1}{8}$" hard solder pin

Turn 8 for each cock

24: Wrought-Iron and Enamel Murals

Fighting cocks

DRAW the cocks full size with a piece of chalk on to a mild steel sheet or on the floor of the workshop. Find the length of $\frac{5}{16}$-inch square mild steel bar required to make the body and main tail feathers by tracing round the working drawing with a piece of string or wire. Begin to form the shape of the cock by starting at the beak.

Mark off the bar and centre pop the position. Heat this area with a brazing torch or on the forge. Place the centre pop mark on a bottom fuller in the anvil and strike with a hammer to form a crease and spread the metal on the inside of the bend. Reheat in the forge and bend; form the acute angle by striking with a hammer on the anvil. The shape of the body can now be easily bent cold. This bending can be simplified by placing two pieces of $\frac{1}{2}$-inch round mild steel rods in the vice. Drop the square bar in between and gently ease and coax the bar to shape. Check the bending by comparing with the master drawing.

Where the square bar crosses at the tail a halving joint should be made and the joint brazed. Form the three supplementary tail feathers from $\frac{1}{4}$-inch square mild steel and braze into position. The comb and wattle are made from $\frac{1}{8}$-inch round mild steel and are held in position by drilling four $\frac{1}{8}$-inch holes and hard soldering.

The wall fixings should now be made by turning, or forging, and the back of the cock drilled and the fixings brazed or hard soldered into position.

By allowing the cocks to project forward from the wall a shadow will be formed with the room lighting, giving an interesting pattern and a feeling of depth to the mural.

The supports for the enamels should be made from $\frac{1}{8}$-inch round mild steel and hard soldered in position as in previous project.

Enamel the tail feathers brilliant blues, green, and red. The head is enamelled ivory and shaded with brown and yellow. Enamel the comb and wattle red.

Paint the cocks matt black and wire the feathers in position.

The background for our mural at school is made from a sheet of hardboard 8 feet × 4 feet, strengthened at the back with a wood frame made from 2-inch × 1-inch deal.

Two or three coats of cream emulsion were painted over the surface.

The cocks are held in position by pushing the pins through holes drilled in the hardboard and bending down on the back.

Cat

The effectiveness of this decoration is achieved by its simplicity of line and the contrast of the three enamels highlighting the face.

Make the cat from $\frac{1}{4}$-inch square mild steel, following the procedure for making the fighting cocks.

Form a halving joint at the top of the nose and ease this forward to project about 1 inch. Projecting the nose forward helps to give some feeling of depth to the features.

Mount the cat on hardboard, a wood panel, or direct on to the wall.

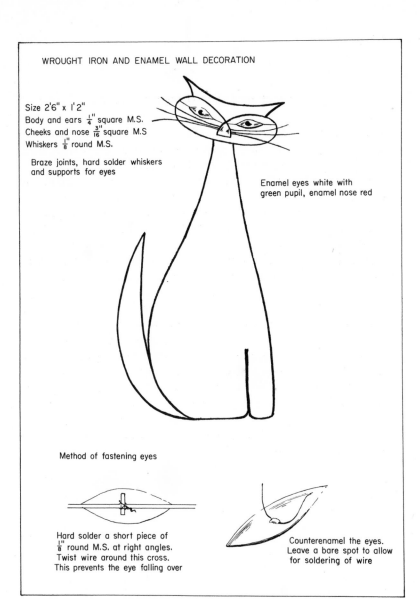

WROUGHT IRON AND ENAMEL WALL DECORATION

Size 2'6" x 1'2"
Body and ears $\frac{1}{4}$" square M.S.
Cheeks and nose $\frac{3}{16}$" square M.S
Whiskers $\frac{1}{8}$" round M.S.

Braze joints, hard solder whiskers
and supports for eyes

Enamel eyes white with
green pupil, enamel nose red

Method of fastening eyes

Hard solder a short piece of
$\frac{1}{8}$" round M.S. at right angles.
Twist wire around this cross.
This prevents the eye falling over

Counterenamel the eyes.
Leave a bare spot to allow
for soldering of wire

25: *Carved Wood Mask with Enamel Inlay*

ENAMEL can be used as accents of colour with other media such as wood sculpture. The carved masks illustrated are made from hardwood, with coloured enamels inlaid flush with the surface.

Draw the outline of the mask on to the face-side of the wood, and cut out with a bow-saw.

The mask can be held for carving by means of a G clamp, a bench clamp, or by gluing a block of wood on the back and holding in a vice. Mark the main lines of the features and carve with a mallet and gouge. Refer to the side-view of the mask for the shape to carve, and leave the tip of the chin, nose, and forehead, at the full thickness of your wood.

Cut your shapes for the enamels from thin card and then cut from 20 SWG copper sheet. Shape the copper to fit the form and enamel in bright colours. Place your enamels on the mask, trace round them with a sharp pencil or scriber. Carefully cut along the traced line with a sharp penknife or chisel.

Remove the surplus wood by means of a chisel, starting from the centre and working to your cut.

Glue the enamels in position with 'Araldite' or 'Bostik'.

The masks are fitted flush to the wall by means of two nails or by making a keyhole slot.

CARVED WOOD MASKS ENAMEL INLAY

Size 12" x 7" x 2" Sycamore

Use 20 S.W.G. copper for enamels. Enamel in bright opaque colours, use impact adhesive or Araldite

Fit flush to wall by means of a keyhole slot or drive 2 nails head first into back of masks. Allow them to project $\frac{5}{8}$"

Size 9" x 6" x 2" Mahogany

Place screw into hand drill, revolve the screw and press down at the same time

Making a keyhole slot

Drill hole the diameter of screw head

Cut a slot the diameter of the screw shank

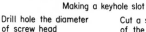 

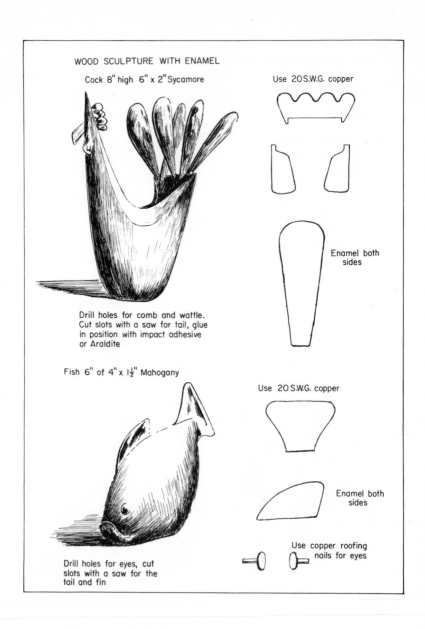

WOOD SCULPTURE WITH ENAMEL

Cock 8" high 6" x 2" Sycamore

Use 20 S.W.G. copper

Enamel both sides

Drill holes for comb and wattle.
Cut slots with a saw for tail, glue
in position with impact adhesive
or Araldite

Fish 6" of 4" x 1½" Mahogany

Use 20 S.W.G. copper

Enamel both sides

Use copper roofing
nails for eyes

Drill holes for eyes, cut
slots with a saw for the
tail and fin

26: Metal Sculpture

Bird form

MANY fascinating pieces of metal sculpture can be made by building with small diameter square and round M.S. bar. The bars can be welded or brazed, and various grades of hard solder used for adding the different parts. The main line of the bird is drawn on a mild steel sheet and the $\frac{1}{4}$-inch square bar bent by means of the two round bars held in a vice.

Make the tail from $\frac{3}{16}$-inch square mild steel bar, and weld or braze in position.

Shape the $\frac{1}{8}$-inch round wire by bending round lathe chucks or the beak of the anvil.

Fasten the rings in position with binding wire and hard solder.

Hard solder a small piece of $\frac{1}{8}$-inch rod to form a cross where the eyes and wing are to be wired in position. This will form an anchor-point for your wire and prevent the enamels from twisting.

Forge and bend the legs and join the two pieces together with a halving joint and braze.

Wire the legs to the body and hard solder.

The beak is made from $\frac{1}{4}$-inch square bar and a $\frac{1}{8}$-inch shoulder and pin is filed on one end and a pyramid shape filed to form the beak.

Drill a $\frac{1}{8}$-inch hole in the main frame and hard solder the beak in position.

Paint the bird matt black and wire the enamels in position.

Jonah

This project illustrates the use of sheet metal to form your piece of sculpture.

The problems of design and the development of the metal can be determined by the use of thin card.

The whale is cut from 22 SWG mild steel sheet or from 20 SWG copper. Drill the holes for the rivet and support.

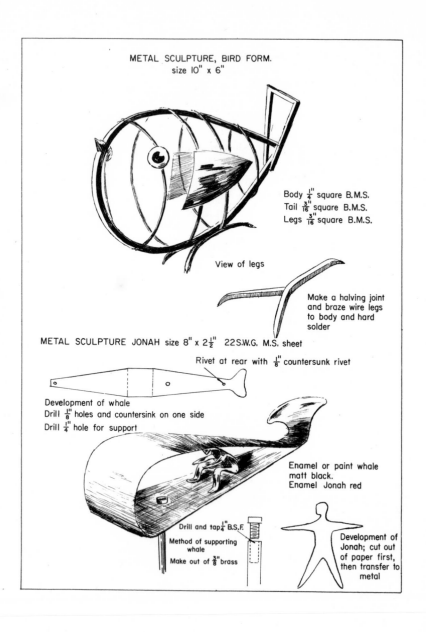

METAL SCULPTURE, BIRD FORM.
size 10" x 6"

Body $\frac{1}{4}$" square B.M.S.
Tail $\frac{3}{16}$" square B.M.S.
Legs $\frac{3}{16}$" square B.M.S.

View of legs

Make a halving joint
and braze wire legs
to body and hard
solder

METAL SCULPTURE JONAH size 8" x 2$\frac{1}{2}$" 22S.W.G. M.S. sheet

Rivet at rear with $\frac{1}{8}$" countersunk rivet

Development of whale
Drill $\frac{1}{8}$" holes and countersink on one side
Drill $\frac{1}{4}$" hole for support

Enamel or paint whale
matt black.
Enamel Jonah red

Drill and tap $\frac{1}{4}$" B.S.F.

Method of supporting
whale

Make out of $\frac{3}{8}$" brass

Development of
Jonah; cut out
of paper first,
then transfer to
metal

Bend the shape and rivet at the tail with a $\frac{1}{8}$-inch countersunk head rivet.

Cut Jonah from sheet metal, bend to shape, and enamel in opaque red. Leave bare metal by masking with paper at the points to be soldered. Place Jonah in position in the whale and soft solder at the points of contact.

Should you enamel the entire sculpture you will have to hard solder Jonah in position before enamelling.

The brass support is made by drilling, turning, and tapping on a lathe.

The base consists of a $4 \times 4 \times 2$-inch wood block.

Beetle and fish

These are two further projects in metal sculpture and enamel, and are built up in a similar way to the bird sculpture.

After making these metal sculptures you will no doubt create your own designs from natural forms.

Insects make ideal subjects to base your designs on. They can be made as large as you wish and the enamels fired in brilliant colours.

These projects in sculpture have measurements to give you a guide as to their size, but the use of a ruler is not necessary, in fact it should be discouraged. The boys who made these pieces used no ruler at all in the making, but sketched them freehand on the workshop floor and shaped the metal by rule of hand and eye.

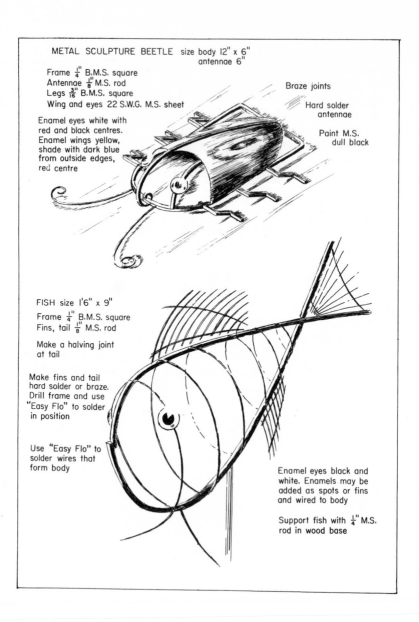

METAL SCULPTURE BEETLE size body 12" x 6"
antennae 6"

Frame $\frac{1}{4}$" B.M.S. square
Antennae $\frac{1}{8}$" M.S. rod
Legs $\frac{3}{16}$" B.M.S. square
Wing and eyes 22 S.W.G. M.S. sheet

Enamel eyes white with
red and black centres.
Enamel wings yellow,
shade with dark blue
from outside edges,
red centre

Braze joints

Hard solder
antennae

Paint M.S.
dull black

FISH size 1'6" x 9"

Frame $\frac{1}{4}$" B.M.S. square
Fins, tail $\frac{1}{8}$" M.S. rod

Make a halving joint
at tail

Make fins and tail
hard solder or braze.
Drill frame and use
"Easy Flo" to solder
in position

Use "Easy Flo" to
solder wires that
form body

Enamel eyes black and
white. Enamels may be
added as spots or fins
and wired to body

Support fish with $\frac{1}{4}$" M.S.
rod in wood base

22   *Cock; wood sculpture with enamel*

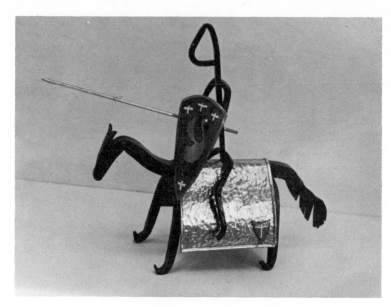

23   *Knight in mild steel with enamel*

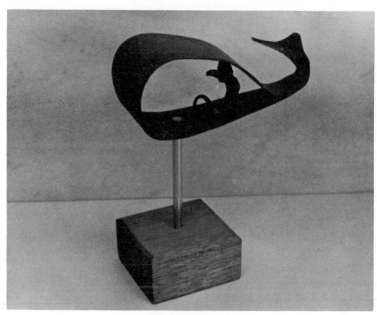

24   *Jonah: metal sculpture*

116

27: The Enamelling of Steel

THIS section on enamelling of steel is written in the simplest terms for the craft enamellist.

Many books and articles are available on the use of enamel for the commercial production of domestic and industrial appliances in vitreous enamel. It is not intended to enter into the complexities and theories of the milling and compounding of enamel for mass production, but to describe how to enamel the surface of steel in the craft-room with limited equipment.

Enamelling steel

Mild steel can be enamelled, but for the little extra cost enamelling quality steel should be used.

The surface of the enamelling steel has a bright granular textured surface and is covered with a thin film of oil to prevent oxides forming.

In industry degreasing of large quantities of metal for enamelling is achieved by the use of caustic soda or trichlorethylene baths. For the purpose of enamelling steel as a craft the simplest way is to remove the oil with a paraffin-rag, scrub with pumice-powder, then rinse with water and dry with a clean cloth.

The grease can also be removed by grease burning.

This method was used extensively in industry until it was superseded by the use of degreasing baths.

Place the metal in the kiln for a period of 1 to 2 minutes at 800° C. Remove from the kiln and allow to cool slowly. Do not quench the hot steel sheet in water or it will result in distortion, which is undesirable, especially if the steel is in the form of tiles.

The pickle-bath

When the metal has cooled hold with a pair of steel tongs and place in a pickle-bath comprising 10 PARTS WATER and 1 PART HYDRO-CHLORIC ACID.

The bath should be of glass, earthenware, or polythene, and

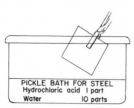

PICKLE BATH FOR STEEL
Hydrochloric acid   1 part
Water   10 parts

Polythene tank

Degrease tile by preheating in kiln at 800°C for 1–2 mins. Allow to cool. Place in acid bath for 10–20 mins. Remove from tank and rinse well in water

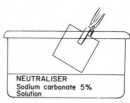

NEUTRALISER
Sodium carbonate 5%
Solution

Polythene tank

After rinsing in water, place tile in neutraliser for 5 mins. Remove from tank and rinse in water. Dry the tile

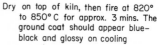

Steel may be handled provided your hands are free from grease and oil

Immerse tile in ground coat. Remove and allow to drain. Hold tile as shown; this allows surplus enamel to drain off the edges

Dry on top of kiln, then fire at 820° to 850°C for approx. 3 mins. The ground coat should appear blue-black and glossy on cooling

Immerse tile in cover coat and drain. Allow to dry and fire at 820° to 850°C

have a lid fitted. Do not put hydrochloric acid into a lead-lined tank as the acid will attack the lead and seepage of the acid will result.

Observe the same precautions when making this pickle-bath as those required for making the copper pickle. ADD ACID TO WATER.

Using tongs, place the steel in this bath for a period of 20 minutes.

On removal the steel should have a bright granular appearance.

Rinsing

To remove any residual acid on the steel rinse under running water.

Neutralization

The steel now requires to be immersed in an alkali to neutralize any acid that may remain in the surface of the metal.

The neutralizer consists of a solution of 0·5 per cent sodium carbonate in water. The tank should have a lid and be similar in size to the one containing the pickle.

After rinsing in water the steel should be placed in the neutralizer for a period of 5 minutes.

Using tongs remove the steel from the bath and rinse in water. Allow the steel to dry on top of the kiln or dry with a paper towel.

Unlike copper prepared for enamelling, steel may be handled provided your hands are not greasy or covered in oil, as it has no effect on the fusion of steel enamels.

Preparation of Steel Enamel

Steel enamel is prepared commercially for the spraying and dipping of domestic and industrial ware by grinding enamel frit and other materials with water in a large ball-mill that is revolved slowly for several hours.

The ball-mill consists of a steel cylinder lined with silica, and it is half-filled with flint pebbles or porcelain balls.

Other materials added to the enamel frit are ball clay to hold the enamel in suspension and electrolytes such as sodium nitrate to prevent the enamel tearing when fired.

Due to the complexities of balancing a steel-enamel formula it is advisable to leave the grinding of steel enamel to the expert. Prepared steel enamel can be purchased at a reasonable cost from commercial enamellers.

28: Enamelled Steel Tiles

STEEL tiles can be used individually for inlaying in wooden coffee-tables or several can be used to make an enamelled table-top, or for the making of murals.

The marking out of the tiles must be accurate. Should you have welding equipment, the corners need not be cut but can be welded.

Steel enamels will fuse over a weld but not a brazed joint. To ease the task of bending, the corners are cut at 45 degrees before the tiles are flanged.

The edges are beaten down by means of a jig or on the hatchet stake.

Tiles have been successfully made out of 24 SWG M.S. sheet with no flange, but these are liable to warp when fired. However, the tiles can be cramped down on to a wood base with a piece of wood across the tiles and G cramps.

The steel tiles should be prepared for enamelling by following the instructions on pages 117–19.

Steel enamel is purchased in liquid form and is similar in consistency to clay made into slip.

The baths we use in school for holding the enamel are square plastic washing-up bowls with a loose-fitting wood lid.

You will require two bowls, one for the ground coat and one for the cover coat.

Ground-coat enamel

To enamel steel, it is necessary to fire a ground coat on to the surface.

The ground coat is blue-black in colour and is specially made to fuse to steel surface and form a ground for the cover-coat enamels.

Stir the ground coat thoroughly and ensure that there are no lumps. Immerse the tile in the enamel.

Remove the tile from the bath and hold as illustrated, allowing the surplus enamel to drain back into the bath.

The ground coat should not be too thick, but have the

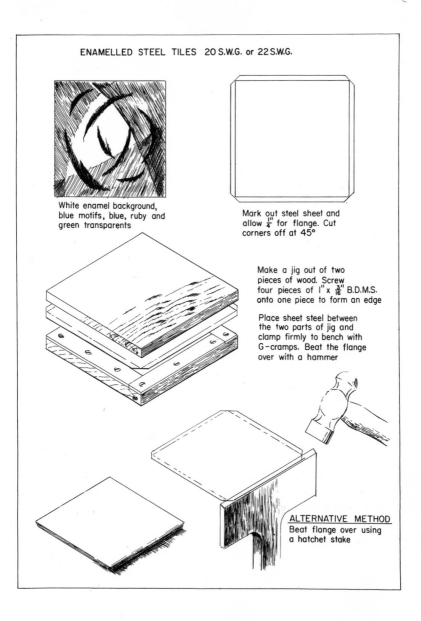

ENAMELLED STEEL TILES 20 S.W.G. or 22 S.W.G.

White enamel background, blue motifs, blue, ruby and green transparents

Mark out steel sheet and allow $\frac{1}{4}''$ for flange. Cut corners off at 45°

Make a jig out of two pieces of wood. Screw four pieces of $1''$ x $\frac{3}{16}''$ B.D.M.S. onto one piece to form an edge

Place sheet steel between the two parts of jig and clamp firmly to bench with G-cramps. Beat the flange over with a hammer

ALTERNATIVE METHOD
Beat flange over using a hatchet stake

I2I

appearance of fine wet sand when draining off the tile. In the event of the enamel thickening, add cold water slowly and stir until it has the consistency of paint.

Place the tile on a stilt made from stainless steel and dry on top of the kiln.

Any pinpricks or tiny lumps of enamel in the surface of the dry enamel can be smoothed down by gently rubbing with your finger.

Firing

When the tile is dry, place two firebricks on the table and rest the tile by the edges to form a bridge between the bricks.

Wear a pair of asbestos gloves and place the firing fork under the tile with one hand and lift.

Open the door of the preheated kiln with the other hand and place the tile on the Perritt points.

Remove the fork and close the door.

With a little practice you will be able to load the kiln in one smooth operation and prevent excessive heat loss.

The firing temperatures of steel enamels are in the region of 820° C to 850° C.

We preheat the kiln to 900° C for firing steel enamel as there is a 50° C heat loss when loading the kiln.

After 2 minutes check the enamel by looking through the peephole.

The tile is enamelled when it appears red-hot with a reflecting surface.

An 8-inch steel tile requires approximately 3 minutes to fuse the enamel.

When the tile has fired, put on a pair of asbestos gloves, remove the tile from the kiln by means of the fork, and place across the two firebricks and allow to cool.

The ground coat should appear glossy and blue-black in colour.

Avoid underfiring the ground coat, as you will have difficulty in refiring. The enamel will probably scale off if you refire the tile, due to the difference in expansion of the underfired enamel and the steel.

Cover-coat enamels

When firing steel enamels, especially cover-coat enamels that are

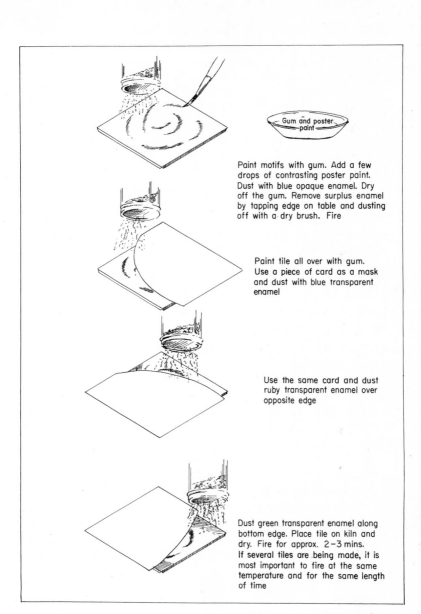

Gum and poster paint

Paint motifs with gum. Add a few drops of contrasting poster paint. Dust with blue opaque enamel. Dry off the gum. Remove surplus enamel by tapping edge on table and dusting off with a dry brush. Fire

Paint tile all over with gum. Use a piece of card as a mask and dust with blue transparent enamel

Use the same card and dust ruby transparent enamel over opposite edge

Dust green transparent enamel along bottom edge. Place tile on kiln and dry. Fire for approx. 2–3 mins. If several tiles are being made, it is most important to fire at the same temperature and for the same length of time

to match with one another as in a coffee-table-top, it is important to make a note of the kiln temperature (by means of a pyrometer), and of the length of time required to fire the tile.

Cover coats can vary in colour with different firing times.

Cover-coat enamel can be obtained in either glossy or matt finish and in a wide range of colours.

The enamels we use in school are a titanium white gloss enamel and a matt black. These two enamels cover most of our needs because we can obtain a wide range of colours by firing jewellery enamels on top of the steel enamel.

When the ground-coated tiles are covered with the white enamel the surplus is allowed to drain back into the bath.

Should you have a streaky surface after draining, hold the tile flat and gently shake. This will help to distribute the enamel evenly over the surface.

Allow to dry on the kiln and then fire, following the same procedure as for the previous firing.

Decoration with jewellery enamels

Jewellery enamels will not fire direct on to steel, but will fire easily on to the steel-enamelled surface.

Use opaque enamels for your ground colours and motifs and then use transparent enamels for the interchange of colour and to add depth to your tiles.

Paint the motifs in gum to which a few drops of poster-paint have been added to make it visible against the light background. Dust with enamel.

Dry the gum on top of the kiln, and, holding the tile by the edges, tap the edge on the table to remove the surplus enamel.

The edges can be tidied by means of a brush.

The tile should now be fired.

After the tile has cooled, paint the surface with gum and dust the transparent enamels evenly, using a card for a mask. This should be done as quickly as possible before the gum has time to dry.

Dry off the gum and fire as before.

Fitting tiles to a flat surface

The method used in industry for bonding enamelled steel sheets to various backings is by the use of an impact adhesive and the panels put under pressure.

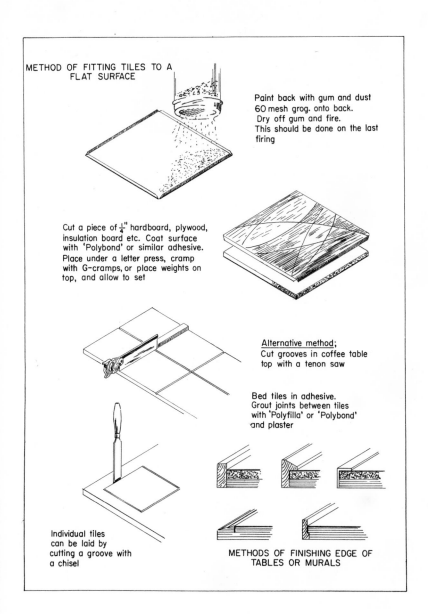

METHOD OF FITTING TILES TO A
FLAT SURFACE

Paint back with gum and dust
60 mesh grog. onto back.
Dry off gum and fire.
This should be done on the last
firing

Cut a piece of $\frac{1}{4}$" hardboard, plywood,
insulation board etc. Coat surface
with 'Polybond' or similar adhesive.
Place under a letter press, cramp
with G-cramps, or place weights on
top, and allow to set

Alternative method;
Cut grooves in coffee table
top with a tenon saw

Bed tiles in adhesive.
Grout joints between tiles
with 'Polyfilla' or 'Polybond'
and plaster

Individual tiles
can be laid by
cutting a groove with
a chisel

METHODS OF FINISHING EDGE OF
TABLES OR MURALS

To form a key on the enamelled surface for the adhesive, on the last firing a mixture of 60s grog and enamel is sprayed on the back. Grog is the term for earthenware that has been fired and ground, which is used in the making of pottery.

This key can be formed on the background by dusting the grog on to gum and firing into the enamel.

Our experience of fitting tiles to coffee-tables, etc., has shown that with the use of 'Polybond' or 'Cascorez' adhesives, it is possible to glue tiles without the use of grog.

The diagrams show various methods of fitting the tiles to the top.

Glue the tiles on the base in sections, starting at one end. Place a board across the face of the tiles and a board under the base and cramp down with G cramps and leave for at least $\frac{1}{2}$ hour, then proceed with the next row of tiles.

The joints between the tiles should be grouted with 'Polyfilla'.

 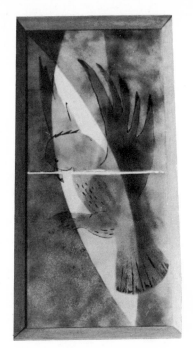

25 'Bottles'; coffee-table-top in enamelled steel tiles

26 Tray: two 8-inch steel tiles with design in transparent enamel

27 Matt black steel enamelled fish

29: Coffee-Table in Enamelled Steel Tiles

THIS project shows one method of enamelling a table-top in opaque and transparent jewellery enamel with the aid of a stencil.

Coat the white enamel tiles with gum, using a large brush or spraying with a garden spray.

Place two bottle shapes cut out of paper in position, give a light spray of gum and dust with opaque blue enamel.

Carefully remove the paper shapes, dry the tiles, and fire for an equal length of time and at a similar temperature.

Place the tiles in position and spray with gum. Use a stencil of two more bottles and dust with transparent enamels. Dry the tiles and fire.

Repeat this stage again with another stencil of two more bottles.

COFFEE TABLE IN STEEL TILES

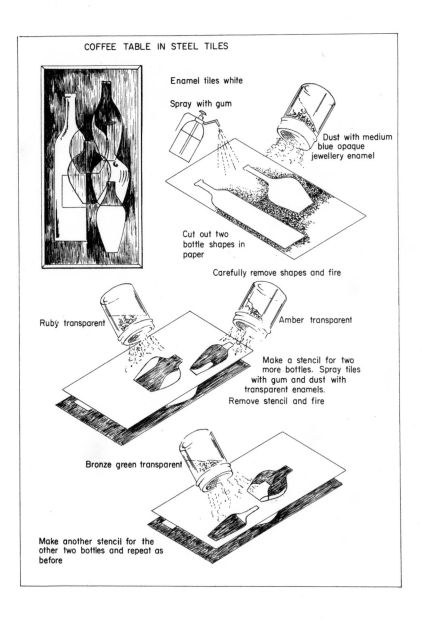

Enamel tiles white

Spray with gum

Dust with medium blue opaque jewellery enamel

Cut out two bottle shapes in paper

Carefully remove shapes and fire

Ruby transparent

Amber transparent

Make a stencil for two more bottles. Spray tiles with gum and dust with transparent enamels.
Remove stencil and fire

Bronze green transparent

Make another stencil for the other two bottles and repeat as before

30: Screening Enamels

VITREOUS enamels are available in various colours in the form of paint. These are used commercially for the silk-screen printing of signs.

The enamels are suitable for use in schools for the screen printing of tiles and for direct painting on steel and jewellery enamels.

It is important that the enamel should be dry before firing, and it requires firing for approximately 1 minute at 800°C.

28   8-inch steel tiles in matt black enamel

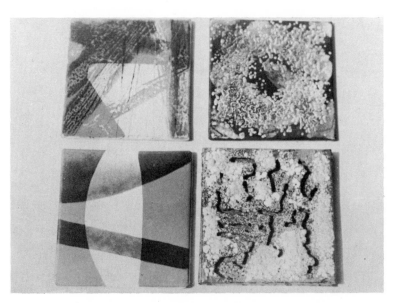

29   Examples of textures on 8-inch square steel tiles

30 *Enamelled bird in steel, 10 inches long*

31 *Coffee-table-top in 8-inch enamelled steel tiles*

32 *Loading an 8-inch steel tile into a kiln*

31: Designs

A SELECTION of designs has been included in this book for the purpose of giving the reader a starting-point in designing for enamel-work, and to act as a stimulant and encourage the creation of your own designs.

You should visit museums and art galleries and explore what has been done in the past by artists and craftsmen, and what is being done by our craftsmen today. Observe how they have overcome the problems of designing for a functional purpose, and how they have used decoration.

The page of Greek designs was taken from pottery made in 600 B.C. and yet today they are acceptable in our modern society because of their simplicity of form.

Study natural forms, collect photographs, clippings from magazines, and make sketches until you have a collection of your own designs from natural form.

The brush drawings are designs for the use of overglaze enamelling. They illustrate how motifs can be achieved with a simplicity of tone and line. Practise these drawings on paper using a Chinese brush and ordinary writing ink. These brushes are reasonable in price and are ideal for this type of work. Work freely, and do not be afraid of making a mistake. With practice you acquire the feel of the brush and draw lines with ease.

The last designs are of shapes for brooches, pendants, and ashtrays that have been made by my pupils in the workshop.

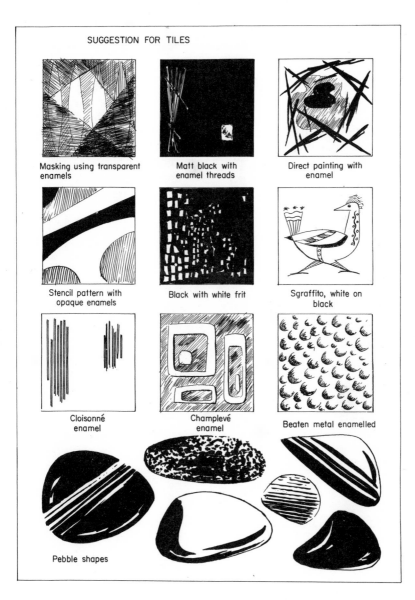

SUGGESTION FOR TILES

Masking using transparent enamels

Matt black with enamel threads

Direct painting with enamel

Stencil pattern with opaque enamels

Black with white frit

Sgraffito, white on black

Cloisonné enamel

Champlevé enamel

Beaten metal enamelled

Pebble shapes

32: Suggested Projects in Enamel

Woodwork

Mosaics and inlay · Firescreens
Coffee-table tops · Table-mats
Trays · Paperweights
Boxes · Lamp-bases
Book-ends · Wood sculpture

Metalwork

Ashtrays · Boxes
Serviette-rings · Bowls
Mobiles · Plates
Metal sculpture · Table-tops
Murals · Lamp-bases
House numbers · Door-handles

Light Craft

Jewellery · Tie-clips
Brooches · Bookmarks
Pendants · Name-tags
Necklets · Medallions
Bracelets · School crests
Ear-rings · Buttons
Cuff-links

Greek 600.B.C.

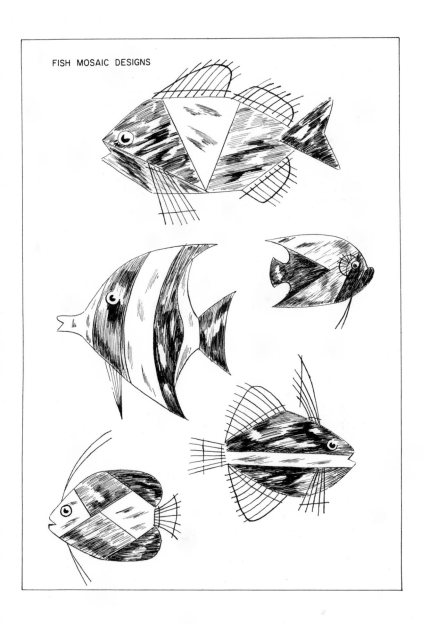

FISH MOSAIC DESIGNS

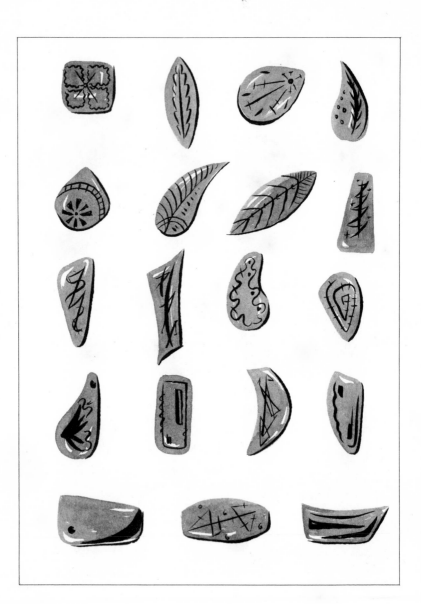

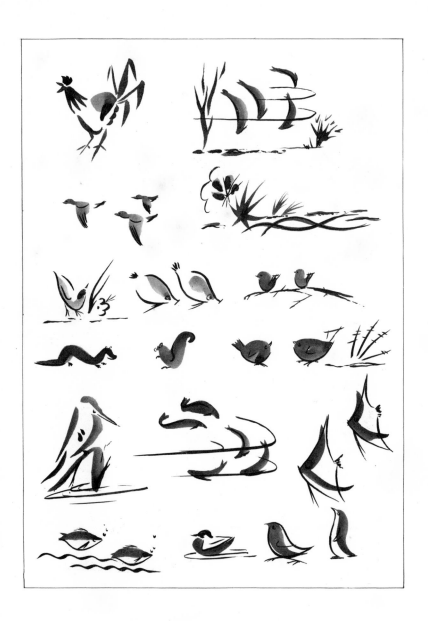

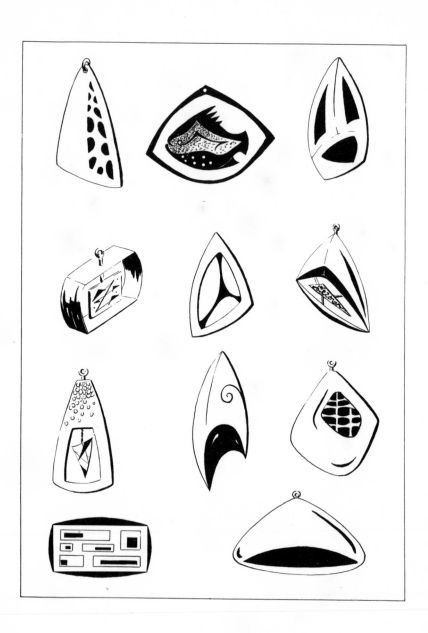

Tables

1. GAUGES

No.	S.W.G.	Birmingham Metal Gauge	Brown & Sharpe American Gauge
		Decimals of an inch	
1	·300	·008	·289
2	·276	·009	·257
3	·252	·010	·229
4	·232	·012	·204
5	·212	·014	·182
6	·192	.016	·162
7	·176	·019	·144
8	·160	·021	·128
9	·144	·024	·114
10	·128	·028	·102
11	·116	·032	·090
12	·104	·035	·080
13	·092	·038	·072
14	·080	·043	·064
15	·072	·048	·057
16	·064	·051	·050
17	·056	·055	·045
18	·048	·059	·040
19	·040	·062	·036
20	·036	·065	·032
21	·032	·069	·028
22	·028	·073	·025
23	·024	·077	·022
24	·022	·082	·020
25	·020	·090	·018
26	·018	·100	·016
27	·016	·112	·014
28	·015	·124	·012
29	·014	·136	·011
30	·012	·150	·010

148

2. MELTING-POINTS OF SILVER SOLDERS

Extra easy	680°–700° C
Easy	705°–723° C
Medium	720°–765° C
Hard	745°–778° C
Enamelling	730°–800° C

Bibliography

Title	Author	Publisher
ENAMEL ART ON METALS	Edward Winter	Chapman & Hall
ENAMELLING PRINCIPLES AND PRACTICE	Kenneth F. Bates	World Publishing Co.
ENAMELLING ON METAL	Oppi Untracht	Pitman
ENAMELLING ON METAL	Millinet	Technical Press
METALWORK AND ENAMELLING	Herbert Maryon	Chapman & Hall
JEWELLERY AND ENAMELLING	Greta Pack	Technical Press
THE DESIGN AND CREATION OF JEWELLERY	Robert von Neumann	Pitman
METALWORK AND ITS DECORATION BY ETCHING	O. Almeida	Mills & Boon
METAL SMITHING	Richard Thomas	Pitman
METAL SCULPTURE	John Lynch	Studio Books
MOBILE DESIGN	John Lynch	Studio Books
YOUR JEWELLERY	J. Leslie Auld	Sylvan Press

Addresses of Suppliers

Materials	Suppliers
Prepared Steel Enamels	W. G. Ball Ltd, Anchor Road, Longton, Stoke-on-Trent, Staffs.
Jewellery Enamels	W. G. Ball Ltd, Anchor Road, Longton, Stoke-on-Trent, Staffs.
	Blythe Colour Works, Cresswell, Stoke-on-Trent, Staffs.
	W. J. Hutton (Enamels) Ltd, 285 Icknield Street, Birmingham 18
Enamels and all Sundry Equipment	Wengers Ltd, Etruria, Stoke-on-Trent, Staffs.
Kilns and Accessories	Arts & Crafts Unlimited, 49 Shelton Street, London W.C.2
	Cromartie Kilns Ltd, Park Hall Road, Longton, Stoke-on-Trent, Staffs.

Kilns	R. M. Cotterson-Smith Ltd, Adam Bridge Works, Wembley, Middlesex.
Perritt Points and Nickel Chrome Bar	W. G. Ball Ltd, Anchor Road, Longton, Stoke-on-Trent, Staffs.
Enamelling Kits	Bernard W. E. Webber Ltd, Webcot Works, Alfred Street, Finton, Stoke-on-Trent, Staffs.
	E. J. Arnold & Sons Ltd, Craft Suppliers, Butterley Street, Leeds 10
	Enamelaire, 61B High Street, Watford, Herts WD1 2DJ
	Alec Tiranti, Charlotte Street, London, W.1
Information and List of Suppliers for Calor Gas	Calor Gas (Distributing) Co. Ltd, 178–202 Great Portland Street, London, W.1
Panning Metal	W. J. Hutton Ltd, 285 Icknield Street, Birmingham 18
	Sankey Green Wire Weaving Co., Thelwall, Warrington, Lancs.
Copper Gilding Metal Sheet and Bar	William Gabb, 127 Barr Street, Hockley, Birmingham

	J. Smith & Sons (Clerkenwell), 50 St John Square, London
	Tuckers (Sheffield) Ltd, Shoreham House, Shoreham Street, Sheffield 1
	Matbrit Ltd, Highfield Road, Manchester 19
	London Metal Warehouses, Summer Road, Thames Ditton, Surrey
Stainless Steel List of Stockists from	Firth-Vickers Stainless Steels, Staybrite Works, Sheffield 9
	Samuel Fox & Co. Ltd, Stocksbridge Works, Sheffield
Gold, Silver Jewellery Findings, Silver Solders	Johnson Matthey & Co. Ltd, Vittoria Street, Birmingham 1
	Sheffield Smelting Co. Ltd, Royds Mill Street, Sheffield 4
Etching Materials	T. N. Lawrence, 2–4 Bleeding Heart Yard, Greville Street, Hatton Garden, London, E.C.1
Polishing and Finishing materials for Metal, Acid-Baths, etc.	W. Canning & Co. Ltd, 77 St. John Street, London, E.C.1
	Also at
	Great Hampton Street, Birmingham 18

Tools, Jewellery

E. Gray & Sons Ltd,
3 Clerkenwell Road,
London, E.C.1

Thomas Sutton (Birmingham) Ltd,
166 Warstone Lane,
Birmingham 18

Charles Cooper,
12 Hatton Wall,
London, E.C.1

Index

Abrasives, 19
Acid bath, 48
Acid resists, 48
Adhesives, 23, 37, 126
Aluminium, 19
Annealing, 34, 40

Bassetaille, 60–2
Beads, enamel, 84–5
Bezel-cutting, 64–5; setting, 81–2
Brazing equipment, 23, 39;
    hearth, 84
Burning out, 25, 50

Champlevé, etching method,
    46–51, 57–8; with gilding
    metal, 53
Cloisonné, traditional, 68–70;
    simplified, 72–3
Copper, 18, preparation of, 19,
    30; protection of, 51
Copperheading, 18
Counter-enamelling, 22, 31, 66–7

Degreasing, 19, 46
Designs, sources of, 134 et seq.
Drawplates, 68
Dusting, 31

Eyes, enamel, 84–5

Findings, 34
Firescale, 87
Firing, 23; under-, 83, 86; over-,
    83, 86
Flux, 15, 34

Frit, 15, 20, 34
Fusion, 31, 34; points, 50

Gilding metal, 18, 19; designs
    with, 53
Gold, 18
Grease-burning—see degreasing
Grog, 126
Gum—see Adhesives

Jewellery enamel, 15, 16, 20–23;
    contamination of, 31; matur-
    ing-point, 31; uses on steel, 124

Kilns, 25; supports, 26–7
Kits, enamelling, 25–6

Lustres, 83

Mitres, 64, 68
Mosaics, 96–99
Metal preparation, 19, 20, 30
Metal sculpture, enamel with,
    111–13

Overglaze enamel, 78, 80
Oxides, removal of, 19, 34, 42
Oxidization, prevention of, 44;
    uses of, 51

Panel making, 65
Paraffin wax, 57
Pickle-bath, 20
Pickling—see Oxides, removal of
Pitch, 74, 76
Pitting, causes of, 35; prevention
    of, 31

155